KIRK

—| *and* |—

ANNE

LETTERS OF LOVE, LAUGHTER, AND A LIFETIME IN HOLLYWOOD

Kirk and Anne Douglas
with MARCIA NEWBERGER

RUNNING PRESS
PHILADELPHIA

© 2017 The Bryna Company
Published by Running Press,
An Imprint of Perseus Books, LLC,
A Subsidiary of Hachette Book Group, Inc.

Books published by Running Press are available at special discounts
for bulk purchases in the United States by corporations, institutions,
and other organizations. For more information, please contact the
Special Markets Department at Perseus Books, 2300 Chestnut Street,
Suite 200, Philadelphia, PA 19103, or call (800) 810-4145, ext. 5000,
or e-mail special.markets@perseusbooks.com.

ISBN 978-0-7624-6217-9
Library of Congress Control Number: 2017931956

E-book ISBN 978-0-7624-6218-6

9   8   7   6   5   4   3   2   1
Digit on the right indicates the number of this printing

Designed by Susan Van Horn
Edited by Cindy De La Hoz
Typography: Neutra, Bauer Bodoni, and ITC New Baskerville

Running Press Book Publishers
2300 Chestnut Street
Philadelphia, PA 19103-4371

Visit us on the web!
www.runningpress.com

If you're a movie star you get all the credit.
But my wife deserves more than half. To my wife Anne,
this book is dedicated to you. —KD

This is the story of an unending love affair.
For my husband and friend, Kirk. —AD

contents

foreword by Michael Douglas *6*

introduction *9*

CHAPTER ONE: WHEN WE WERE YOUNG *11*

CHAPTER TWO: OUR COMPLICATED COURTSHIP *31*

CHAPTER THREE: 1954: OUR ROMANCE GOES TRANSATLANTIC *45*

CHAPTER FOUR: TOGETHER AT LAST *65*

CHAPTER FIVE: BRYNA'S EARLY YEARS *77*

CHAPTER SIX: 1957: ON LOCATION IN ARIZONA, GERMANY,
    AND NORWAY *89*

CHAPTER SEVEN: FACING DIFFICULTIES AT HOME *101*

CHAPTER EIGHT: BECOMING SPARTACUS *121*

CHAPTER NINE: OUR HOLLYWOOD LIFE *133*

CHAPTER TEN: A LIFE BEYOND HOLLYWOOD *153*

CHAPTER ELEVEN: FRIENDS IN HIGH PLACES *171*

CHAPTER TWELVE: FRIENDS AND FAMILY *189*

CHAPTER THIRTEEN: CARING IS SHARING *205*

afterword *221*

foreword

by MICHAEL DOUGLAS

THE SECRET TO A GREAT PLAY IS ITS THIRD ACT. If the audience is still engaged by the story, enthralled with the characters, and surprised by what it sees, the playwright has created magic.

Kirk and Anne is a book overflowing with magical stories. Their life together has been filled with romance and drama, great triumphs and heartbreaking tragedies, and a glamorous Hollywood lifestyle. If their letters reveal anything about Kirk and Anne Douglas, it is that from the very beginning they were opposites who could not help but attract. Each of them brings out the very best in the other.

My father Kirk wears his heart on his sleeve, while Anne protects hers with a caution borne of bearing life's burdens with dignity and strength. Yet it is that very protective quality that makes her the lioness that she is. She's used it to take care of all of us, especially my father. I remember as a young boy, after my father and my mother Diana divorced, not only did Anne treat my brother Joel and I as though we were always a family, she invariably showed great love and respect to our mother. With Anne's characteristic dry wit, she referred to her as "our ex-wife."

In their third act, Kirk is still enthralled by Anne, as she is by him. My father recently told me, "Cole Porter loved Anne." Think of it: a young woman from France, newly arrived in Hollywood in the early '50s and married to one of the world's biggest movie stars, is invited to accompany her husband to a dinner party hosted by the legendary lyricist/composer. It is the star's young wife, with her European style and effortless grace, who delights their host. She is invited back and told, "You may bring your husband too, if you must."

This book begins with the passionate and poignant story of their courtship as revealed through their never-before-published letters. It then follows their seven-decade journey through happiness and hardship, annotated by their correspondence with the influential and remarkable people who have shared that journey with them.

If this book is the curtain for their third act, I can't wait for their fourth.

—Michael Douglas, January, 2017

introduction

MOVIE DIRECTORS CALL THE FLEETING MOMENTS when sunset approaches the "magic hour." Some of the most memorable moments in film history have been shot in the last light of day. In our house, we celebrate it as the "golden hour"—a time to reflect and connect, to recall and relive some of the magic hours that have filled our enduring union of more than sixty years.

When we reminisce about our courtship, we could never have imagined our new love growing into a lifetime of these golden hours. Some of them have followed painful, heartbreaking days. We made it through even the hardest of them because, at the end, we had each other.

One evening when we were sitting in front of the fire in the great room of our Montecito home, I, Kirk, asked my wife if I had ever sent her love letters. She smiled mysteriously at me. "Would you like to see them?" she asked. "I'll be right back." She returned with a battered-looking manila file folder filled with flimsy air mail envelopes, letters on pages from the yellow-lined legal pads we used at home, and dashed-off notes on odd slips of paper—some of them the kind of billets-doux that lovers write "just because."

I, Anne, have very few mementos from my early life before Kirk. In the turbulent years before and during World War II, I moved from Hannover to Brussels and then to Paris, taking only essentials each time. As a result, the letters and memorabilia of our life together were even more important to me.

My main repository for the collection has been the climate-controlled wine cellar of our Beverly Hills home, which I call the "dungeon." It is filled with boxes of letters and photographs from friends and fans, from Hollywood royalty and political leaders all over the world. Most harken back to a kinder, gentler time, when writing notes in one's own handwriting was considered a mark of courtesy. I admit the handwriting on some of them is hard to decipher, mine included.

The intimate letters of our courtship and marriage have been hidden for many years—in a secret spot in my Montecito bedroom. I haven't looked at them since I put them there, but they are very precious to me. I saved whatever Kirk wrote me, of course, but over the years I also collected my letters to him. I would find them in the suitcases I unpacked when he came home from locations. I was happy to share them again with Kirk.

As the golden hour faded into darkness that evening, we read a few of them aloud to each other in front of the fire. We both had forgotten how intensely we communicated after we fell in love in Paris in 1953, married in Las Vegas in 1954, and endured subsequent separations because of film commitments. In addition to the long newsy letters, there were cables, notes scribbled in airplanes and between takes, and a few X-rated ramblings about how much we missed each other. It was like seeing them for the first time all these years later.

I, Kirk, have written eleven books over the years, some of them autobiographical and three since I turned ninety. Now in the beginning of my one hundredth year, I felt there was nothing new to say about my life or the people in it. For several years I had toyed with the idea of writing a book of letters, based on the ones Anne had stashed in the dungeon. I couldn't find the right thread for a cohesive narrative and lost interest. Suddenly I knew the missing ingredient: it was Anne. I had written about her many times, but how extraordinary to read how she felt about her life with me—its opportunities, its drawbacks, its pleasures and pains.

I looked at my wife. "I'll tell you what's in here," I said, tapping on the precious file before me. "It's *our* book."

—*Anne and Kirk Douglas, April 2016*

CHAPTER ONE

When We Were Young

KIRK:

I know little about my immigrant parents' early life in Russia. *Fiddler on the Roof* is a sanitized version of their *shtetl* world at the dawn of the twentieth century. During a pogrom, my mother, Bryna Sanglel, saw a Cossack murder her brother. She had no pleasant memories of the Old Country—at least none that she ever shared. After I became the Hollywood star, Kirk Douglas, and Ma was living comfortably in the Jewish Home for the Aged in Troy, New York, she worried I would go to Russia. Her reaction was strong and immediate. This is from her letter of April 8, 1958, which she dictated to my sister:

> *Dear Anne and Kirk,*
>
> *I have heard from several people that they have heard about your (Kirk) being invited by Russia to make a picture there. This came as a big shock to me and I pray to God that while I am alive you will not go to Russia. I do not mind whenever and wherever you go elsewhere but not to Russia. Please keep this in mind as I am not young nor too well any longer and these are my feelings. We are happy and proud of whatever you do and we have heard too much unfavorable news about Russia to have you embroiled there.*
>
> *Stay well and happy and write again soon.*
>
> *My dear son, God bless you.*
>
> *Love, Mother*

We had no relatives in America except for my uncle Avram. He arrived a year before my father, and changed his name from Danielovitch to Demsky. Pa—Herschel Danielovitch the horse trader—became Harry Demsky the ragman after joining his brother in Amsterdam, New York. Pa was very strong, but the thriving local factories would not hire Jews. He bought a horse named Bill and a cart so he could buy old rags, scrap metal, and any other junk lying around people's homes. He took the day's haul to a dealer for pennies on the pound. The next year he sent a steerage ticket for his young bride. Whether he paid for it himself I highly doubt. My father spent his earnings on drink in the nearest saloon. Without that ticket, my sisters and I would never have been born.

I don't know if my parents loved each other or whether their marriage was the work of the local *shadchen* (matchmaker). I never saw a sign of affection between them. Pa never addressed my mother by her name, Bryna. It was usually, "Hey you." All I know for sure is that Ma bore him seven children between 1912 and 1924. I, Issur Danielovitch, fourth in line and the only boy, was born on December 9, 1916—one hundred years ago. The others were Pesha (Betty), Kaleh (Kay), Tamara (Marion), Rachel (Ruth), and the twins, Hashka and Siffra (Fritzi and Ida). When I reached school age, I was enrolled as Isadore (Izzy) Demsky—a name I always hated.

Yiddish was the only language I heard in the house. Until I was old enough for kindergarten, I did not play with other kids on the street. They were a polyglot mix from many countries. Their fathers worked in the factories. During the days, Ma and I inhabited a world of our own. I liked it that way. With only cold water in the kitchen, a washboard for her laundry, and no icebox (not that we ever had much to store in one), Ma was constantly cooking, cleaning, washing clothes, and worrying about paying the bills. Pa was no help. Almost all his daily take was spent at his favorite bar, Bogie's. He rarely came home for dinner. He never seemed to care whether we had food on the table or went to bed hungry.

We lived in abject poverty. My wife always tells people, "Kirk hates to hear anyone say they were poorer than he was." She's right. I am proud of it, because it made me hungry to achieve success. I told my

Isadore and Bryna Demsky in Amsterdam

sons, "You didn't have my advantage. From the bottom there's only
one place to go. Up!"

But as a toddler, with no other experience to judge our living standards by, I was content to bask in Ma's delight with me. She loved her
daughters, but I was her prince. My sisters never seemed to mind,
because my mother told them not to expect too much of life. "Girls are
dreck (shit)," I heard her say more than once. For sure, Pa reinforced
that belief. Then again, he didn't treat me, his son, any better.

By the time my fourth birthday rolled around on December 9, 1920,
women had just cast votes for the first time in an American election.
The nineteenth amendment to the Constitution had finally been rat-
ified by Congress that August. It didn't mean anything to my mother,
who couldn't read a newspaper, even in Yiddish. It wouldn't have
changed her view on a woman's role in the universe. In Amsterdam's
small Orthodox synagogue, she prayed with others of her sex in the tiny
upstairs balcony where she could barely see the Holy Ark below.

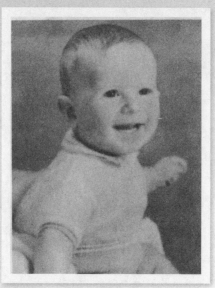

Baby Izzy

Outstanding Pupils

FROM TOP: *Baby Issur, 1916; "Outstanding pupil" Izzy (top left) with other kindergarten classmates; Izzy's (bottom row, extreme right) stage debut as a sailor in the kindergarten play* Christopher Columbus

Production - Christopher Columbus

While my three older sisters were at school, I had Ma all to myself. I loved being in the warm kitchen on a cold winter day, watching her roll out the challah dough. On Friday night, the braided loaf would sit on the *Shabbos* table alongside the candlesticks that had been passed to her from her mother. I own them now. This ritual ushered in Ma's only day of rest, a sacred interval from dusk on Friday until three stars could be seen in the sky on Saturday.

In the kitchen at age four, I plied her with important questions while she worked:

"Ma, how was I born?"

"Issur, you arrived in a gold box from heaven."

"Wow! What did you do?"

"I ran outside and wrapped you in my shawl."

"Did you take the gold box, Ma?"

"No. I only wanted what was inside, *myne kind.*"

———————| ★ |———————

In kindergarten I entered a strange new world with an unfamiliar language. I enjoyed being there and having friends my own age. Before I knew it, I was speaking English. When I recited a poem about the red robin of spring, everyone clapped. I took my first bow before an audience. I loved it. By second grade I was a seasoned pro, milking my title role of the shoemaker in *The Shoemaker and the Elves.* My mother and my sisters, of course, were there. My father said he would not come. Pa took zero interest in any of us children. But I was surprised. There he was, standing with his back against the exit doors. He didn't say much, but he bought me a loganberry juice before taking me home. The memory is as fresh to me more than ninety years later as the night it happened. I had longed for him to give me a pat on the back. This was the closest he ever came to it. Even when I was a famous movie star, he never told me he saw any of my films. I heard later that he bragged about me to his drinking friends.

Why was he like that? I can only guess. Perhaps he had believed the myth that American streets were paved with gold bricks. I saw another side of him one night at Bogie's. Looking into the window of the saloon, I watched him. He was in his element, a natural actor with a rapt audience of bar cronies hanging on his every word.

When I had my Bar Mitzvah at thirteen—impressing the small congregation with my delivery of the Hebrew text and my speech in Yiddish—I got a few gold pieces as presents. I had been earning money by delivering the Schenectady newspaper to subscribers scattered all over town. It would have been much easier to deliver the *Amsterdam Evening Recorder*. I couldn't get a route because I was Jewish.

Together with what I had saved from my job and my Bar Mitzvah, I now had a college fund of $313. I handed it over to my father when he asked to borrow it, even though my mother begged me not to. I think I wanted him in my debt. Pa bought a lot of metal he was going to sell for a good profit. It was just before Black Tuesday, on October 29, 1929. The price of metal plummeted. My college fund was gone, and I never heard another word from him about it.

By the time I was in high school, I was sure I wanted to be an actor. My English teacher, Mrs. Livingston, befriended me and didn't belittle my dreams. "To be a great actor, you have to be a great person. You must be educated. You must be trained," she said. I sent away for college and drama school catalogs.

I began to write poetry and had good roles in the school plays. In my junior year, I won the Gold Medal in the Sanford Prize-Speaking Contest. My sister Marion had won it two years earlier. My oldest sister, Betty, never had a chance to enter. She left school in the ninth grade to go to work. She was our sole support during the leanest years of the Depression.

In my senior year, Mrs. Schuyler, the drama teacher, organized a class trip to see Katharine Cornell in Albany, starring in *The Barretts of Wimpole Street*. Who could have predicted that the first time I stepped on a Broadway stage I would deliver a singing telegram to Grace George in *Spring Again*, a drama produced by Guthrie McClintic, Katharine Cornell's husband. I was included in the cast invitation to their grand home off Beekman Place for Thanksgiving. It was the first time I tasted champagne and caviar.

There were 322 of us in my graduating class of 1934. I won the Best Acting and Best Speech Prizes as well as one for my essay, "The Play's the Thing." My mother and sisters were there. My father was not. With no money for college, I worked for a year in men's ready-to-wear at the M. Lurie department store. Then, with $164 in my pocket, I hitchhiked to St. Lawrence University with my friend Pete Riccio, who was going into his sophomore year.

I took all my awards and transcripts with me. Dean Hewlitt interviewed me and took a chance on this insolvent applicant reeking of manure from our last hitch on a fertilizer truck. Today the Dean Hewlitt Building on campus sits directly across from the Kirk Douglas Building. I have never forgotten my debt to the university and to the man responsible for my being there. For many years now I have funded full scholarships for minority students; I feel good to be giving them the chance I had.

I found acceptance at St. Lawrence despite some blatant examples of anti-Semitism. The top fraternity wanted to pledge me when they thought I was Polish. The invitation went away when they discovered I was a Jew. I was elected class president, a really big deal, at the end of junior year. Rich alumni threatened to cancel their checks if the Jew took office. Once again, Dean Hewlitt championed me. I was what they called a BMOC (Big Man on Campus)—class president, undefeated star of the varsity wrestling team, president of the Mummers Club, president of the German Club. I had no trouble getting dates with the most popular coeds.

Meanwhile, my mother and sisters had moved to another house. Pa remained alone on Eagle Street. After my sophomore year, I went to Amsterdam to see them before starting my summer job, wrestling for money in a carnival. I stopped first to say hello to Louise Livingston and to Pa. He was surprised to see me walk in the house. He put down the garlic and herring he was eating; he served me a piece with a glass of vodka. We ate in silence. Then he beckoned me to join him as he headed to his regular haunts. I was thrilled. It was the dream of my childhood to be initiated into his world. By the time he delivered me to Ma hours later, I was drunk and disoriented. She cursed Pa in Yiddish when she saw the state I was in. She worried I would follow in his footsteps.

As I became more and more fixated on being an actor, I spent the next summers at the Tamarack Playhouse on Lake Pleasant in the Adirondacks. I was a stagehand, but pushed to get onstage. I started with a few small parts, with a promise of bigger ones to come.

At first I was billed as Isadore Demsky. "That won't do," said my new friends Karl and Mona Malden. "That's not a proper name for an actor." Karl had started out as Mladen Sekulovich in the steel town of Gary, Indiana. One boozy night, Karl and Mona convened a group of us in their cabin to look for my new name. I emerged hours later, reborn as Kirk Douglas. It was 1939. A man named Adolph Hitler was sending German armies to conquer countries in Europe. I only wanted to conquer Broadway.

I knew I needed more training and was accepted at the American Academy of Dramatic Arts in Manhattan. I made some lasting friendships there. One was Betty Bacall, a stunning seventeen-year-old who had a crush on me. Another was Diana Dill, who was always telling Betty to forget about me.

Betty was renamed Lauren when Howard Hawks brought her to Hollywood to star in *To Have and Have Not*. And Diana married me after I joined the navy in 1942. We became swept up in the romance of wartime and the fear that I might die in combat.

After four months of training at Notre Dame midshipmen's school, I was assigned to PC1139, an antisubmarine patrol craft, as a communications officer. I looked great in my dress uniform, but nothing else about my service was distinguished. With a green crew and a captain who had never been to sea, we were one of the most incompetent ships in the navy. Our first time out of port in New Orleans, we backed into another ship and almost sank it. Then, on our first sighting of a Japanese submarine in the Pacific, a nervous sailor released a depth charge instead of a depth charge marker and blew us up. I was bruised and had internal injuries. Then I became deathly ill with severe cramps and a high fever which turned out to be amoebic dysentery. At the San Diego Naval Hospital, I was an inpatient and then an outpatient for several months prior to my honorable discharge in June 1944.

FROM TOP: *Kirk (left) in Tamarack Playhouse production George Washington Slept Here • Young naval officer in peak shape for war*

Before leaving for New York, I was surprised to find out that Lauren Bacall was in Los Angeles. We met for dinner. Betty was still filming *To Have and Have Not* and was living with her costar, Humphrey Bogart. She told Bogie to take me along to the studio the next morning. I was very impressed as I watched him on set, and he couldn't have been more charming to me.

But doing live theater was still my goal. I got good roles in a lot of bad plays, so I readily accepted producer Hal Wallis's offer to costar with Barbara Stanwyck and Van Heflin in *The Strange Love of Martha Ivers*. He came to see me in *The Wind Is Ninety* after Lauren Bacall, now the toast of Hollywood, told him I was a great actor who was getting rave reviews. Betty was my first agent—and I didn't have to pay her a commission.

That's how I moved west and became a movie star. Diana and I had two sons—Michael and Joel—by the time we divorced and she returned to New York. I worked and played hard and enjoyed liaisons with some of the golden age's brightest stars, among them Marlene Dietrich and Gene Tierney, as well as a beautiful oil heiress named Irene Wrightsman. Then, I fell in love with a young Italian actress, Pier Angeli, when we were trapeze artists in a film called *The Story of Three Loves*.

With my family to support and taxes under Eisenhower sky-high, I took my lawyer Sam Norton's advice to make films abroad for the next eighteen months. One of them was *Act of Love*, where I met Anne Buydens. Her story is more dramatic than mine. I'll let her tell it to you.

ANNE:

Kirk was already a famous star when I met him in Paris in 1953. His acting career had taken off in Hollywood, and he had earned Oscar nominations for two of his memorable roles, first in *Champion* and a few years later in *The Bad and the Beautiful*.

When Kirk came to Europe to star in *Act of Love*, I had already turned down Anatole Litvak, the director of the film, to do publicity for it. I went to America instead for the premiere of John Huston's *Moulin Rouge*. I had worked closely with the flamboyant director as a location scout and assistant for more than a year and was thrilled to be going to

Hollywood. It was a dream come true. Crossing the Atlantic by ship, I saw my first Kirk Douglas film, *The Big Trees*. I was not impressed. I could not have imagined that within a few months of seeing it, I would meet Kirk and embark on the fascinating relationship that would lead to our happy marriage of sixty-plus years.

Kirk and I could not have come from two more different worlds. He was a poor American boy from a tiny town in upstate New York, speaking only Yiddish until he entered school. In contrast, I was born to Siegfried and Paula Michelle Marx in Hannover, Germany, one of the most cosmopolitan cities in the country. We were rich and well-traveled. By the time I was in boarding school in Switzerland, I could speak German, French, and English.

My parents named me Hannelore but called me Peter because they had wanted a boy. When I was three, my English governess—whom I hated—took me to the barber for a haircut. "Cut Peter's hair," she said. He obliged, snipping away my bountiful blonde curls and leaving me with a boy's cut, close to my scalp. Some traumas you never forget. This was my earliest.

Kirk adored his mother, Bryna, who loved him unconditionally. He was largely ignored by his father. My relationship with my parents was just the opposite. My beautiful mother, who was very social, didn't take much interest in my daily life. On the other hand, my father wanted to know all about my everyday activities. He bought us a special little blue book where we exchanged little notes on the days when he worked late hours and came home past my bedtime. I would leave him a note about my day. In the morning I would immediately look to see what he had written back.

By the time I was four or five, Papa would talk to me about business. He owned large textile stores in the city. He also was the exclusive importer of an unusually strong silk which the government bought to make parachutes. I took our talks very seriously and was thrilled when he would take me along to visit the shops. One of the sales girls, Trude, made a big fuss over me. She made us matching "friendship bows" to wear on our clothes. I thought she was wonderful.

Anne's parents: Paula Michelle (in Switzerland) and Siegfried Marx

We lived in a spacious three-story house in a beautiful neighborhood surrounded by woods. My sister Ingeborg and I shared the third floor, along with whichever governess we hadn't yet tortured into quitting. But we both liked Trulla, who was more like an older friend. She taught us manners and how to dress and kept us from fighting with each other. Inge was six years my senior. She took after my mother both in looks and her love of luxurious things. I was more like my father.

Kirk was one of seven kids. While he shared a bed with his oldest sister until he was old enough to sleep on the living room couch, Inge and I had spacious bedrooms, a large playroom, and a bathroom with a toilet and two sinks in our private domain. Once a week, Trulla took us for a bath in my mother's rooms on the second floor. She had the most wonderful bathtub. My mother had exquisite taste and the funds to indulge in the best of the best. I remember the streamlined Packard convertible she drove to her many social engagements.

On Wednesday evenings, my parents entertained at home. All day the household staff—the cook Itze, the laundress, the maids—would prepare for the party. Then decorators came in. I liked to sit at the top of the stairs to watch the guests arrive.

That was before my parents divorced. My mother bought a house in Switzerland and kept a chic apartment in Berlin. Inge was in the Swiss boarding school, which I would also attend within a few years. I didn't miss them. I had the ones I truly loved, my father and Trulla, in the house.

My relationship with my father was very important and had a lasting effect on my life. Honesty was paramount to him. Once I told a lie and he paddled me on the behind. I never told another one. I felt I had to live up to his very high standards.

I was content with my life. My father would go on business trips, but Trulla and I always had fun and I was also going to the little local school. Then, suddenly, things changed. I have vivid memories of the day it happened. I was so happy. Papa was coming back from his latest trip. Something was odd. No one said anything to me, but with my ears open I could hear the servants saying, "The poor girl. The poor girl."

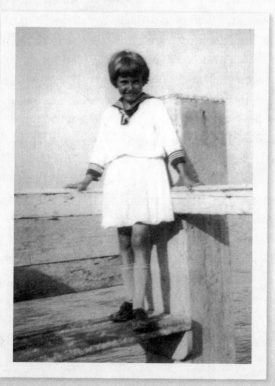

Hannelore (Anne), age four, on holiday by the sea

As usual, I was waiting for Papa by the steps that led from the main floor to the entrance. When I heard the car pull up, I flew down the six stairs to throw myself in his arms. Instead, he stood there with his arm around my friend Trude from the store. The first words out of his mouth were, "Meet your new mother."

I was shocked. I turned around and ran up to the third floor and cried my heart out. Nobody came to console me except Trulla. From that moment my ability to trust was damaged. My father was the man I believed in totally, and he disappointed me completely. Our relationship was never the same because he had lied about Trude and about his business trip. I now felt that, no, you cannot trust anybody.

Kirk and I, once again, are opposites in this. He is all trust, and I am all verify. Over the years, I have suspected some of his closest associates of taking advantage of him. Sadly, I have always been right. Perhaps that's one good thing that came out of my experience with my father.

From then until I went to school in Switzerland, I shuttled between my mother and father. In my mother's elegant Berlin apartment, there was only one bedroom, so I slept on a divan in her dressing room. There was always a man in her life, and at one point she married a Swiss citizen. I don't think it was a love match and it didn't last long.

I was relieved to be boarding with different children from many countries. I spoke in three languages and learned to get along in any situation. That independence helped me to survive when the privileged world of my childhood disappeared in a world engulfed by war.

My father's marriage to Trude didn't last. Nor did his life in Germany. He moved to Switzerland, too, enjoying its neutrality and the money he had prudently placed in one of the banks. Inge had gone on from her Swiss finishing school to become a journalist, writing society gossip for magazines. I didn't see her much.

Although both my mother and father were now in Switzerland, I would visit them separately. During this time, their best friends from Hannover, two brothers named Wallach, decided to move to neutral Belgium. They were taking their young niece with them, a girl about my age. My father readily agreed that I should go along as her companion. I was so used to being shunted around that I was happy for a new adventure.

I lived comfortably with the well-to-do Wallachs until I was fifteen and they left for America, just ahead of the German invasion. Now that the Nazis had conquered Poland and Czechoslovakia, it was only a matter of time before we were next. In May of 1940 the bombs started falling in Brussels.

It was time to get out of Belgium. I left with my friend Albert Buydens and his older brother Leon, a prominent attorney, and another lawyer. There were four of us in the car. We would cross the border into France and meet Leon's wife and the rest of her family in La Baule. The plan was to drive down to Hossegor, a little town just before the Spanish border, where the grandmother of Leon's wife owned a house.

It was chaos on the roads. We weren't the only ones trying to escape. But I was the only one with German papers, which put all of us in danger. When the survival instinct kicks in, you find in yourself a bravery you could never have imagined. Three times at the Belgian and French borders, I shuffled the passports back and forth so deftly the guards never caught on that mine wasn't among them. Once we got to Bordeaux, Leon suggested Albert and I marry to alleviate the problem. It was only to be for a year, and then we would divorce. But the German Army arrived just after we did, and it was just weeks later that the whole of France surrendered. It was no time to be alone in the world, and I was grateful to be with Albert and his family. I was now Anne Laure Buydens, a Belgian national.

For a brief time we thought of crossing into Spain, but the grandmother was not well enough to become a refugee. It would be better, we decided, to sit out the war in Paris, where the family owned property. But how would we get there? To travel, we needed official permits. And only the army had gas.

I had had a prior experience with the German general of the region, who was a decent man. One of the soldiers in his command had raped the grandmother's maid in the woods, and Grandmama insisted I demand his punishment. The general convened a hearing. When the soldier admitted the act, the officer stripped him of his rank and medals.

He wanted to personally apologize to the grandmother.

"What can I bring her?" he asked me.

"She really needs lettuce for her turtle," I said.

Within hours, he came to call, a large case of green lettuce in his arms. Now I was counting on that spirit of generosity to help us leave Hossegor.

I drove one of the cars, perilously low on petrol, to his headquarters. I explained that we had three vehicles, a great deal of family, plus the maid, a bird, and the well-fed turtle to transport to Paris. Could he give us the proper documents, and could we have enough gas to get there safely? He gallantly filled up the tank in my car, wrote out the travel passes, and had some soldiers load huge jerry cans of fuel into the backseat. We had more than enough for the trip. We reached Paris a few days before the Nazis occupied the city. Until the Allies liberated us four years later, we survived as best we could, trying not to break any of the myriad rules imposed on residents. It was a surreal existence in the midst of privation, fear, and snatches of normalcy.

Here is what I remember: you could recognize the officials and soldiers if they wore uniforms, but there were spies and undercover agents all around. Once again, I thanked my father for inadvertently teaching me to be suspicious of everyone. There were also French citizens who were anxious to be on good terms with the Germans or who sympathized with Nazi beliefs. They could accuse anyone. I learned firsthand how this worked when my cleaning lady denounced me to the Gestapo as a spy. She found all these papers. They looked like code. Every other word was *no, maybe, tomorrow*. There were figures on them she thought was a timetable.

At five o'clock in the morning, I was picked up and taken off to be interrogated. I sat in front of the stern German officer, scared to death because I didn't know why I was there.

"Who are you working for?" he asked.

"A company."

"No, I mean, who are you *really* working for?"

"Sonor Pictures."

Luckily, I could speak German to him directly, without a translator putting a spin on my words. I explained I was in the movie business. Sonor Pictures was an English company that was selling French and foreign movies. I worked for their representative in Paris, writing German subtitles. The Occupation had a restriction that any movie not in German had to be subtitled. I was an absolute beginner who spoke and wrote the languages fluently, so I was well qualified in that sense. But I was poorly equipped for the rest of it. I didn't know how to type. I didn't know how to sit alone in a projection room with a stopwatch. I was taught just the basics: you have so much time for the subtitles in this scene. If somebody is just yawning, you write nothing. That sort of thing—tricks of the trade.

It was actually terribly difficult, especially for someone inexperienced. I worked at least ten hours a day. I had wonderful movies to look at, except I had to stop after each scene, write down the few words of description, and then go on to the next. I had taken my work home. The cleaning lady looked at it and rushed off to police headquarters instead of asking me for an explanation.

I was young. I was pretty. I spoke German. I went home. Others who were falsely accused were not so lucky.

So that was the atmosphere—suspicion and fear. Those feelings stay with you even when the danger is over. I lived among people who were as guarded as I was. Everyone was assumed to have a secret. Finding it out was a potent weapon and might help you survive.

Because of that background, I have difficulty in being what they call a close friend. I am a good friend to others but I find it difficult to confide in people. The war years compounded the problem I already had with trust. You had to be careful about where you were and what you were saying.

But life goes on, even in wartime. People fell in love, had lover's quarrels, married and had children; we went to nightclubs and theater and carried on as well as circumstances allowed. Each night at 10:00, a curfew shut down the city. Being on the streets after that was a very serious offense. We had the famous "last Metro"—the final train of the day

FROM TOP: *Wedding day for Albert and Anne (née Hannelore Marx) Buydens • Celebrating the end of the war, Albert and Anne (second and third from right) at a Paris night club*

at around 9:20 p.m. Everybody raced for it, and we'd all gather at the station. Some people had been to parties and were dressed to the nines, with jewelry and evening clothes. Others looked like bums. We were all thrown together, and in a way it was rather festive and fun.

I owed Albert a lot for what he and his family had done to keep me safe. But I still wanted a divorce. Albert was happy with the way things were, but would not object as long as I paid. Since I earned barely enough to cover our expenses, I stayed legally tied to him until 1953, when I met Kirk. And then Albert and I remained what we had always been—the best of friends.

I was still with Sonor Pictures when the war ended. One day I was asked by my boss to go to London for two days to meet with his counterpart, a Mr. Fraser, to sell French movies. My God! The city looked awful—buildings falling down and holes where others had been. It was probably 70 percent destroyed in the Blitz. Nonetheless, the mood was upbeat, and I had a wonderful time. Mr. Fraser took me to dinner one night and there was a delightful show on the club's stage. A lovely girl was singing and dancing in it. I was really struck by her look. I said to Mr. Fraser: "You know, Colette is looking for her Gigi. That girl could do it." He invited her to our table, and I asked her for some photos and background to take back to France. With excitement, I presented the material to my boss. She would be a perfect Gigi, I told him, and we would be credited for discovering her. He heard me out but never followed up. About five months later, someone else saw what I did in the charming seventeen-year-old Audrey Hepburn. He went directly to Colette.

Years later, when Kirk was in Rome during the filming of *Two Weeks in Another Town* and Audrey was living there with her second husband and her boys, I reminded her of the role I *almost* played in her career. But back then, we were both just finding our way in this brave new postwar world—two multilingual survivors who had, even at our young ages, more than paid our dues.

CHAPTER TWO

Our Complicated Courtship

ANNE

Paris was my adopted home. Because of my ease with languages, all kinds of doors were opening to me. But I had gotten a taste of the film business and I liked it. I would stay late at the office and overhear the bosses' strategy sessions. I absorbed as much information as I could, just as I had done in conversations with my father when I was a child.

In America—with the men back from war and French couture once again setting style trends for the world—NBC approached our company to create a television program called *Paris Cavalcade of Fashion*. I was chosen to produce it. I first had to convince important couturiers to let me film their new designs. My crew and I were at Christian Dior's first fashion show after the war, where he introduced the "New Look." I almost missed the opportunity because my director Robert Capa (who lived in Paris when he wasn't off covering wars for his photo agency, Magnum), was not there.

Quel désastre! Luckily, I knew where to find him—in bed with Winston Churchill's daughter-in-law Pamela, in her hotel room. I drove to their hideaway, flew up the stairs, and banged on the door. "Bobby, it's Anne. Get up now and grab your clothes. You can finish dressing in the car!" (Pamela was far more discreet when she became America's ambassador to France, Pamela Harriman.)

For nearly a year, the segments ran on NBC network stations. They even aired the one we filmed on the sleeper train from Paris to Nice, in which I modeled sleepwear. I went to New York several times and fell in love with America. I was taken to fantastic parties by international tycoons, and I had a wardrobe of designer clothes to wear to them. Then the fashion houses withdrew their cooperation. They believed that American manufacturers were using our programs to make unauthorized copies of the clothes.

I don't recall how John Huston, the director of *Moulin Rouge*, came to contact me to scout locations, secure permits, and be his personal assistant. Maybe I was recommended by someone I had worked with briefly on *The Young Lions*. I had a wonderful time taking Mr. Huston to dusty little antique shops and out-of-the-way places that tourists would never find. He, in turn, introduced me to Pre-Columbian art. A jockey he had known in Mexico was importing ancient pieces from there; John was an avid collector. Almost every night we had dinner together, along with Tony Veiller, who wrote the script for the film. Inevitably, I got sucked into John's colorful private life. Here's how I kept him out of jail.

John was living in a beautiful old house in the French countryside. When the shoot was nearing its end, his wife, Ricki, arrived from St. Clerans, their estate in Ireland. They had me organize a luncheon in the garden the next Sunday. During it, John disappeared with Colette Marchand, the French actress who played a prostitute in the movie. A while

Modeling Dior's New Look for Paris Cavalcade of Fashion

Anne filming Paris Cavalcade of Fashion *with Robert Capa in Deauville*

later, I saw Ricki go upstairs. I know exactly what happened next, because a tearful Ricki told me. She had walked in on her husband with Colette. He jumped out of the bed and put his hands on her shoulders. "Do you believe in me," he asked, "or do you believe in what you just saw?"

A few days later, John got into a fight with Colette's beau, the film's production manager, at a well-known nightclub in Paris. His longtime bodyguard and good buddy pulled out a knife and stabbed the boyfriend. Naturally, the police were called. My phone rang in the middle of the night:

"Anne, they are trying to arrest John Huston and it's not good."

I got up and thought about what I could do. I had a connection with someone at British Airlines, so I contacted him. "I have to get Mr. Huston out of the country before they confiscate his passport and press charges," I pleaded.

"*D'accord*, Anne. Bring him directly to the airport and we'll shove him on to one plane or another. Don't stop anywhere."

That's exactly what I did—little me—saving the famous director from the *gendarmes*. When it came time for the American premiere in December of 1952, Huston asked me to accompany Colette to Hollywood. I was so excited. Seeing Hollywood was such a dream of mine. I stayed at the Hotel Bel-Air and felt like a star myself. The hotel's owner, Joe Drown, took a fancy to me. He took me to a New Year's Eve party in La Quinta.

In California I accompanied Colette to all her press appearances and events. We met with the Hollywood Foreign Press Association, which awarded her the Golden Globe as Newcomer of the Year, and she received a nomination for Best Supporting Actress from the Academy of Motion Picture Arts and Sciences.

When I got back to Paris a few weeks later, my friend Anatole (Tola) Litvak, the director of *Act of Love*, convinced me to meet with Kirk, who was anxious to hire a bilingual assistant who could also handle his personal publicity. I drove over to the studio where Chim Seymour, the still photographer, greeted me with these words: "Let me take you into the lion's den."

Kirk had already gotten quite a reputation in his first few weeks in town. The press had dubbed him *Le Brute Chéri*, the darling brute, and he was photographed with a succession of stunning women. I was sure this would be a courtesy interview. I had signed a three-year contract to handle protocol for the Cannes International Film Festival starting in April 1953; I hoped to go back to the States for a visit before it began.

KIRK:

I was fascinated by the lovely young Parisienne who sat in my dressing room, her slim ankles crossed under her *à la mode* blue suit with white collar. Within minutes, I offered her the job. She took only seconds to turn me down in her impeccable English. I was not used to rebuffs. I walked Anne back to her car and urged her to change her mind. I appealed to her vanity: "I really need your help."

She replied, "It's not for me, but I can recommend a wonderful young man."

A few hours later, in my most seductive tones, I called Anne to invite her to dinner at the romantic La Tour d'Argent, one of the city's most celebrated temples of cuisine.

"Thank you, but I'm tired. I will just make some scrambled eggs and stay in tonight," said the voice on the other end of the phone.

I was shocked and annoyed. I was determined to change her mind—at least about the job. I sent emissaries: Tola Litvak, Irwin Shaw—*Act of Love*'s screenwriter who remembered her from *The Young Lions*—and Anne's friend Robert Capa, who often partnered with Chim Seymour on their Magnum assignments in war zones. She finally agreed to work with me on a trial basis, making it clear our relationship would be strictly business.

We spent a lot of time together. Anne was efficient and had a wicked sense of humor. Everyone liked her—much more than they liked me! We often spoke in French, which I was studying from a method called *Assimil* with Madame LaFeuille two hours a day, six days a week. Tola Litvak was shooting two versions of *Act of Love*, first in English and then in French. Although I was only contracted for the one in English, I relished the challenge of doing both. After all, an American G.I. would speak French with an accent and I had a good ear for languages. At night, after my lessons, I did my "homework" in total immersion with various *mademoiselles*.

With no romance in the picture, I stopped trying to impress Anne. Instead, I stopped talking about myself and began to listen to her. She had told me very little about her background; I didn't even know that she spent her early years in Hitler's Germany. I thought she was Belgian. That all changed one overcast day in February.

ANNE:

Kirk was invited to the annual charity gala at the *Cirque d'Hiver*, the famous Winter Circus, where French celebrities participated in the show. He loved circuses and, of course, had done a trapeze act with Pier Angeli in *The Story of Three Loves*. He wanted me to accompany him.

We had been working through the afternoon at his lovely apartment near the Bois de Boulogne when he started asking me questions about my life. I was always reluctant to talk about myself, particularly as so much of my past was painful.

Kirk was an attentive listener, and I found myself being very honest. I even opened up about my rift with my father and why I had lost trust in him. Kirk was extraordinary. He said I should try harder to understand my father and forgive him. He had spent a lot of hours on the analyst's couch to learn the importance of what he was telling me. We talked for hours, and I had a strange feeling in my heart that I could fall in love with this man.

I didn't want to, because I had seen too many young women enter into intense affairs with visiting movie stars—Dean Martin, Marlon Brando, Cary Grant among them. Then the film wrapped and the men returned to their wives and families. Hadn't I seen it firsthand with John Huston?

At the circus, the producers spotted Kirk coming in. "You must participate," they told him in French, which I no longer had to translate for him. I took my seat, wondering what he would do with no preparation. After the elephants left the arena, there was the tuxedoed Kirk—the popular *brute chéri*—pushing a giant pooper-scooper of a broom across the ring to great hilarity. How could I resist a man who could laugh at himself? We went back to his place for a nightcap, which turned into something more. Once again, my life was changing.

KIRK:

After hearing Anne's story, I understood her resistance to my advances. She was not interested in a frivolous affair. This self-possessed beauty was very different from the women I had been involved with in Hollywood since Diana left me. She wasn't neurotic like Gene Tierney, who always insisted I arrive for our nocturnal "dates" by climbing the tree outside her bedroom window. She wasn't reckless like my much-married oil heiress, Irene Wrightsman, whom I found in our bed with Sydney Chaplin when I came home early from the studio. Anne was a sophisticated woman, unlike my virginal Pier Angeli, who took her mother on all our dates. I was fascinated by Anne and more than a little in love with her.

ANNE:

If this had been a Hollywood movie of the 1950s, it would have ended happily after this revelatory evening. But I knew from hard experience that real life rarely played out that way.

The next day our working relationship had a new warmth. And I started spending more time with him socially. I would stay with him some nights, but I still kept my apartment and my independence. Kirk gave me a key so I could come and go as I liked. He also kept his independence, and I wasn't always meek about it.

This is the note he wrote me after I walked away angry one afternoon. I found it on the table the next morning. I was glad he understood he had hurt me. It was always easier for Kirk to write about his feelings than to talk about them.

> *Darling,*
> *I have a feeling that you're not coming back tonight. I hope I'm wrong!*
> *—It's been a bad day for me and probably a worse one for you. Because my bad day means all of my problems added to yours. Forgive me.*
> *But I hope that you are here to read this and that I find you when I get back.*
> *—Suddenly it seems stupid that I am going to dinner without you—*
> *Because believe it or not I love you!*
>
> *Kirk*

KIRK:

Another thing I learned about Anne the day of the *Cirque d'Hiver* was that she was still legally married to Albert Buydens. She also told me she was involved with a wealthy French industrialist, many years her senior. He didn't help her financially, and, in fact, had never given her anything more lavish than grapes out of season.

Honest and correct in all her dealings, she told him about her feelings for me and broke it off. He treated the news like a business competition. I bought her a small piece of jewelry. He countered with a small car called a Reno. He was positive their relationship would resume after I returned to the States. I understood staying friendly with an ex. Diana and I still enjoyed each other's company.

It had been too long since I had seen my boys. I invited Diana to bring them to Paris and stay in my spacious apartment for a few weeks. The kids had just recovered from chicken pox. A few days after arriving, Diana developed the telltale rash. In her role as my efficient assistant, Anne administered medication and brought her chicken soup. The two women liked each other. Michael and Joel got along with her, too.

As things became more serious with Anne, I warned her not to expect a commitment. I was secretly engaged to Pier Angeli, I told her. I could have saved us both a lot of anguish if I had used my new fluency in French to read the movie magazines. Anne knew, but never breathed a word, that Pier was constantly in the news, always with another man at her side. Meanwhile, whenever I tried to call Pier, I was always told she was traveling with her mother.

My next picture would be filmed in Italy, so I was sure that would all change. The two producers of *Ulysses*, Dino de Laurentiis and Carlo Ponti, were going to the Cannes Film Festival in April and I would meet with them there. They had already hired Anne Buydens to do the unit publicity for the picture. One way or the other, my connection with Anne would continue.

ANNE:

I was in Cannes preparing for the sixth International Film Festival, which would run from April 15–29, 1953. There was no festival during the war years, and it didn't revive until 1947—every other year at first. By 1953 it was once again a glamorous, thriving showcase for international cinema. My job as head of protocol was to work with all the foreign representatives. I organized and scheduled their galas and made sure they were filled with celebrities and media. I shared an office with George Cravenne, a good friend who handled the festival's publicity.

Kirk got a kick out of hearing me switch effortlessly between languages. He studied his script for *Ulysses* on the beach and took publicity shots with the starlets. One of the photos, with him and a bikini-clad Brigitte Bardot, became a tourist postcard. Brigitte had had a small role in *Act of Love*. Kirk had never imagined there were such extraordinary assets hidden under the bulky coat she wore in her scenes. They have stayed friends and just a few years ago Brigitte sent him another of their beach photos, writing, "My dear Kirk: Were we not so nice and young and beautiful?"

AUGUST 2012
My dearest Kirk
Were we not so nice and
youngs and beauty full?
I just wanted send you thors souvenir
so rare and tell you that the animals
and all my Fondation are sending
you our deeply kisses —
B.B. Bette

Fondation
Brigitte Bardot

Reconnue d'utilité publique par décret en date du 21 février 1992

Brigitte Bardot and Kirk at Cannes, 1953

I was glad Kirk was in Cannes, although I didn't have much time for him. In the midst of everything, Joe Drown arrived from California and insisted on taking me to dinner in Monaco. It was a disaster. Joe got drunk and gambled heavily. I left him and went back to my suite at the Miramar Hotel. I called Kirk, who was next door at the Carlton. He had been asleep.

"How was your evening?" he asked.

I burst into tears. "Just awful . . . and it's my birthday."

"I'll get dressed and take you out," he said.

We went to a small café near the beach, and he turned my tears into laughter. It was a wonderful birthday, after all.

When the festival ended, Kirk and I left for Italy. I was uneasy about being on Pier's home territory, but she was making a film in South America.

KIRK:

Carlo Ponti invited us to his villa in the hills above Amalfi before the start of production. We had a wonderful, romantic holiday in an ancient tower that served as their guest quarters. During that magical week, Anne and I would set off in a little rowboat. She would row; I would sing her Italian love songs. We explored Amalfi and Positano and then went to Capri.

Anne said to me, "We are so happy with each other."

"But don't forget I'm going to marry Pier," I reminded her gently.

Ulysses started shooting on May 18, 1953, in the little fishing village of Porto Ercole on the Adriatic. The replica of Ulysses's ship was ten miles away; I swam part of it alongside the launch where Anne would sit reading a book. Sometimes I would water-ski for a mile or two.

Then we moved to Rome to continue filming at Cinecittà Studios, which is where Pier surprised me with a visit to the set one day. We resumed our romance, and Anne moved into a hotel.

I cannot believe how insensitive I was. I asked Anne to come to Bulgari and help me choose an engagement ring for Pier. She did it without a murmur, but she must have been seething inside.

ANNE:

This was a particularly painful period for me. I was planning to visit my father after filming on *Ulysses* was complete. I wanted Kirk to meet him. Papa was impressed that Kirk loved me. He liked his films and his success. We were in Rome when Inge called to say our father was in the hospital with angina. I spoke with his doctor, who assured me he would be fine. He died the next day.

My father had returned to Hannover after the war. Inge was there as well with her new husband. Our former home had been destroyed by Allied bombs, so Papa designed a new residence on the site with three separate flats. He lived on the main level in the largest of them. There was a tenant above, and on the lowest floor he had made a small apartment for his daughter Merle. He never married again, but had a housekeeper who was his mistress. She took everything of value except my mother's Steinway when he died.

Finding out about our half sister was a great shock to both Inge and me. My father had never even hinted of her existence. She didn't know about us either, which was also strange. Merle's mother was Trude, who remarried soon after she left our father.

I met this new sister for the first time when Inge brought her to Paris. We had an instant connection. I don't know if my father was aware of our meeting. Even so, he would never have mentioned it to his daughters. His secrets were a deeply ingrained part of his nature.

One of the things I love most about Kirk is his inability to keep secrets. He once asked me, "Honey, how would you like a surprise party for your birthday?" Kirk never tried to hide his dalliances from me. He told me about them himself because I wanted to hear it from him directly, not via an idle piece of gossip.

Let me explain my attitude concerning this. As a European, I understood it was unrealistic to expect total fidelity in a marriage. In Paris I had known General de Gaulle's driver, who was also his mistress, and many more like her. In more recent times, François Mitterrand's mistress and their children came to his funeral at the invitation of his wife. Only the Americans found it outrageous. Kirk secured my permission before including stories of his trysts in his 1988 autobiography, *The Ragman's Son*. I'm positive his candor helped make the book a major bestseller.

In Italy in 1953, he never hid his feelings about Pier, misplaced as I thought they were. She was the fantasy woman of his dreams, innocent and malleable and adorably provocative. I certainly couldn't compete on that level. But I hoped he would finally see her as the manipulative child-woman she was. With the Bulgari ring in his pocket, Kirk flew to London to propose to Pier on her twenty-first birthday. She said yes. Then he came back to work. At the end of the picture, Kirk hosted a party for the cast and crew, which I had to organize. He acted as if we were still together, and against my better nature, I wanted to believe it.

We took a trip to Brussels before going back to Paris. Kirk wanted to see where I had lived. Albert had returned there to work, and we arranged a dinner with him and his girlfriend. That day I toured the city with Kirk, and he had heartily consumed a large lunch of seafood in rich sauces. By evening he felt ill, and I went to dinner alone. When I returned, Kirk reproached me: "I hope you had a nice time. While you were gone, I had a heart attack. The doctor advised me to see a specialist near Baden-Baden immediately, but we have to take the train. Flying might be fatal for me."

I gently suggested that, given what he'd consumed at lunch, it might just be indigestion. However, Kirk was so convinced of the doctor's diagnosis that I became alarmed.

The German specialist kept Kirk in his examining room for a long time. When he emerged, he sheepishly admitted, "The doctor said he's never seen a healthier specimen in his life. He asked what I ate yesterday. Then he told me I had indigestion."

I smiled, and my healthy specimen and I went out to walk around the town. We passed a kiosk with the latest issue of *Paris-Match* on display. Pier Angeli was on the cover. Kirk looked at it. Then he said, "I'm sorry, Anne, I guess I'm still in love with her."

KIRK:

While I was in Rome, my agent, Ray Stark, and his wife, Fran, had come to visit; so did my lawyer and business manager, Sam Norton, with his wife, Bea. Sam told me I was now officially a millionaire. All of the money he had invested for me in oil wells and other properties had made me rich.

Ray had worked things out with Walt Disney for me to star in his first live-action movie—*20,000 Leagues Under the Sea.* We would film in the Bahamas, Jamaica, and Mexico before going back to the studio in Los Angeles. This was great. I could finish my eighteen months abroad and get my tax breaks before going home to the small house with a pool Sam had bought for me, using the power of attorney I had given him. Fran Stark, a talented interior designer, was furnishing it for me.

I flew back to the States for a few days to spend Christmas in New York with Michael and Joel. I also went to see my father, who was seriously ill in an Albany hospital. He looked frail and frightened.

I was back in Paris for New Year's Eve. I was taking Pier to La Tour d'Argent, just the two of us—no Mama! Over dinner, knowing there were no obstacles to a night of passion, I fell out of love with her. I was bored with the conversation. Also, there was no chemistry between us when we kissed as the clock struck midnight. I broke off our engagement. She returned my ring. I couldn't wait to tell Anne.

ANNE:

I was nursing my broken heart at a friend's lovely hotel in the hills above St. Paul de Vence in the south of France. I left strict orders with my maid in Paris not to let anyone know where I had gone. I tried my best to act cheerful, but I was miserable.

Kirk phoned my apartment after leaving Pier at her hotel, but my maid wouldn't tell him where I was. He went to my flat on rue Lord Byron, rang the doorbell, and broke her down easily. The charm and movie-star looks worked every time. He called the hotel. "It's Kirk on the phone," my friend said. "He told me to tell you he just had dinner with Pier Angeli and they broke up and she gave the ring back and it's finished. You must talk to him."

On their Klosters "honeymoon"

I told him, "Don't do this to me again. I don't want to be hurt anymore." But like my maid, I succumbed. I took the afternoon train back to Paris—back to my love and the possibility of more heartbreak.

We went to Switzerland to ski at Klosters, where our friends Tola Litvak, Irwin Shaw, and Robert Capa were already enjoying the slopes. It was like a honeymoon, just perfect. Kirk had never skied before. But, like everything else, he became very good very quickly. Two weeks turned into four, and I expected 1954 to be a good year.

On our return to Paris, I drove Kirk to the airport. I was still taking care of his business affairs in Paris, and had organized the shipping of his trunk and his new car. He told me he would write, but made no promises of anything more. As I kissed him good-bye at the curb, one of Air France's agents came toward us.

"Mr. Douglas, Pier Angeli is waiting for you in the lobby," she said. I drove off, wondering if I had become just another of those women who foolishly fell in love with an American movie star.

CHAPTER THREE

1954: Our Romance Goes Transatlantic

KIRK:

After spending so much time together in France and Italy, our lives were now playing out on separate continents. By March 1954, *20,000 Leagues Under the Sea* had finished shooting in the Bahamas and had moved on to Jamaica. I was at the Round Hill Hotel in Montego Bay when I received word from my sister that my father was dying.

I had a dilemma; Anne was the only one I could tell. Obviously, the letter would arrive in France well after my decision, but Anne had been my sounding board for a long time. I just felt better writing to her.

> *My darling Anne—*
>
> *I certainly wish you were here with me now. Yesterday I received word that my father is dying. Since then I have sent cables and tried to reach them by phone, but can't reach them. I don't know what I should do. You see, I cannot—if for no other reason but for my children—take a chance on losing out on the 18 month period. Maybe I could get there for a day and come right back, but I don't know what I would accomplish. I have a reservation on a plane for this afternoon and I will*

have to decide within the next few hours.

What a futile feeling it is. I just know this must be the end for him, because, at last word, he was in an oxygen tent with pneumonia.

I just talked to my sister. My father is now feeling better. God! What a constitution he must have! I feel like I've been through a wringer.

Please write to me—Love, Kirk

ANNE:

In today's world of instant communication, only people of a certain age remember the frustrations of an air-mail correspondence. Occasionally, Kirk would cable, and sometimes he would be able to get through to me by phone; but it wasn't ideal to shout intimacies over a line that might have static or an operator listening in.

I wrote more regularly than Kirk at first, but he then began to share more and more of his thoughts with me. He also loved the idea of writing in French, with a little German thrown in now and again to impress me. I was always urging him to write longer letters.

Kirk had a pet name for me—Stolz, the German word for "stubborn." He also used "stolzig" (being stubborn) for the way I got when I tried to cover up my feelings of insecurity. Here's a letter he wrote before leaving Jamaica.

Dear Hannelore,

Tomorrow morning I leave for Havana, Cuba, then to the Yucatán, then to Mexico City and on March 16th I leave for California.

Life here in Jamaica is rather dull. The country is beautiful—a little too tropical for me, and the people are uninteresting. Every morning I get up at 6 to drive about two hours over terrible roads to location. And after work—the drive back!

The director is a wonderful guy and Peter Lorre is a lot of fun. I'm including a snap that someone took of both of us.

You will soon be leaving for the south of France. Do your job, but don't knock yourself out! Have some fun (not too much!)

Yesterday I felt terrible, thought I was getting malaria and I needed you to tell me I only had a cold.

I miss you very much, Stolz, and I want to arrange to see you soon. Let's see what happens when I get to California. I'll write to you from Cuba.

Lots of love, Kirk

Our letters crossed. I had posted mine on March 4, 1954.

Tu t'amuses mon chéri? *[Are you having fun, my darling?] Here is some recent news from Klosters. Mr. Bentley-Dauros reported them from his last skiing weekend. By the way, he is really trying very hard to complicate his life by wooing me seriously.*

Tola and Soph have spent a couple of days. Irwin [Shaw] finally sprained his ankle skiing. The weather is not too good, the place is jammed—40–60 minutes to catch a beer. Madame Suler is in love with you and so is everybody in Klosters—and ich auch *[me too]!*

I am leaving Friday the 19th for Cannes and the Festival. The trip and my whole stay will be distressing. Everything is still so full of memories. My Darling, every moment we spent together is still so very much alive.

I am awfully lonely without you. I know that a separation always embellishes the feelings and I also know that visiting is a perfect and dangerous way to create illusions and distortion. For the moment I am still in the world of reality and I wish it would remain this way!

I am sending the records to Mrs. Ponti with a little note saying that you have asked me to do so before your departure.

Darling, write to me once without being afraid of any-

Anne and Sam Norton in Rome, 1953

thing! Speak to me openly. I did it in my previous letters but I am worried I am stolzig again. You can help me by talking to me and don't think you commit yourself or you hurt me.

Please, I need it. A.

KIRK:

After Jamaica, we moved on to Mexico City and the Yucatán, where my friend Willie Schorr and I enjoyed exploring the Mayan ruins. Then I took him to Acapulco for a long weekend. I wrote Anne this letter from the great impresario Mike Todd's house. He was living with Evelyn Keyes who was, incidentally, one of my ex-flames and an ex-wife of John Huston.

Darling—

I am now in Acapulco staying at a most beautiful little house as the guest of guess who??—Mike Todd and Evelyn Keyes who both send their very best.

Willie is with me. We came down here, stayed at a hotel the first night and then bumped into Mike and Evelyn.

How I wish you were here. The bed next to mine is empty—really and I wish you were in it. Very often I miss you terribly but I hesitate to write about it in my letters for many reasons.

I go back to Mexico City on Tuesday and on Wednesday, the 17th, I leave for California. I hope there will be a letter waiting for me there.

All in all the trip from Jamaica to here was very interesting. Did I tell you about your friend Lobo in Cuba?

There are so many things that I say to you in my reveries that I don't know whether or not I have written it to you.

I saw him once and he was <u>most charming</u>. And how well he spoke of you. There were a group of people there and he talked about you as if you were a mixture of Helen of Troy, Josephine, Cleopatra and the Virgin Mary! Frankly, I have never thought of you as any kind of virgin! He has a very charming house, filled with masterpieces.

I went water skiing yesterday and did very well on two skis, but didn't do very well on one. I'll try again today. The weather is perfect here and the place is very charming. I keep thinking I'm in Italy.

I continued my letter in French:

When I get back, I will write to you always in French. Also, I hope that I will begin again to study with a teacher. Sam told me he has hired a Swiss houseman for me who speaks French and German also. If it's true I will speak French with him.

This evening Mike is giving a grand party here with an orchestra. I will miss you very much, I assure you. I am going to lie down and get up late in the morning.

I will write you when I arrive in California. Tell me everything you are doing and all that is going on in Cannes during the Festival.

Is my film Act of Love *showing in Cannes? And the others? Are you sure you can understand me when I write in French?*

Behave yourself, my darling, and write to me soon.

I love you. K.

ANNE:

I was given the letter when I checked into the Carlton, along with a cable Kirk sent from his new house at 1609 San Ysidro in Beverly Hills. I was glad to hear about his visit with my good friend Julio Lobo, one of Cuba's tobacco barons. I had met Julio when I was in New York on behalf of *Paris Cavalcade of Fashion,* and we subsequently saw each other in Paris on various occasions.

I answered Kirk immediately:

> **Mon Amour,**
> *Arriving here this morning, I found your long letter from Aca-pulco and your cable from San Ysidro! I congratulate you on your French.*
>
> *I am so anxious to know what you think about your house. Please write quickly! I am so sad and lonely here without you. I took that sketch of you with me and to prevent me from getting "stolzig," I <u>nailed</u> you in the frame! If you could only hear how I talk to you each night before I cuddle myself in your arms.*
>
> *Darling, you would have to be proud. Never have you been loved so much and so exclusively. If I don't see you soon I am getting nuts!—*
>
> *I am delighted you saw Lobo. What a crazy idea taking me for a virgin! I might have to do something about this. It will ruin my reputation!!—*
>
> *I got your cable from Mexico. By the way, did you get my letters from Jamaica and my cable for our "anniversary"?*
>
> *How is your Swiss manservant? I hope by now your new car and trunk have arrived.*
>
> *Sweetheart, write to me, call me, come over—do anything. I want to be close to you. I want to be loved and loved—and loved again and again! This is what Doctor Kinsey would call: "A dangerous case of starvation"!*
>
> **Stolz**

I wrote again a few days later:

> **My darling—**
> *Tonight you have to excuse me. I am a bit drunk. A little bit of smoked eel and a tiny bit of vodka did it.*

Welcome home Sweetheart!! I can just see you sitting in that comfortable armchair in front of the fireplace and reading a letter from that little Parisian girl you used to know!

You son of a —! Everything has its limits. So you have been to South America but that is still no reason to change your first name into "Ysidro" and on top of it "Saint."

Chéri, I was so delighted when I talked to you over the phone. You couldn't have made me a greater pleasure!

Before I left Paris, Tola showed me the picture (the French version). I must admit I like this version even better than the other. You are terrific, magnifique, *sensational,* formidable *in French! I was so proud of you I bowed to the very "select" audience for my "man"!*

A friend of mine, Bill Robson, came to Paris to do some T.V. scripts and in a conversation he told me that his kids used to play with yours.

To show you how I trust you—I gave your phone number to a very pretty girlfriend of mine. MICHELINE MUSELIE. She is a lawyer—don't feel frightened—only 29 and very much oo-la-la. *So look, but don't touch!!*

I really have sometimes fantastic instincts. Remember when I wrote to you about a brunette in Jamaica. Of course I didn't know that she was brunette all over!! Today I have my "stolzig" day. I won't tell you that I miss you terribly, that I am longing for you, that I am lonely without you and that I love you so very much!

Billy Wilder will be a member of the Jury in Cannes. Maybe you can let him know that I know a wonderful place to eat Sauerkraut in Antibes!

Give Willie a kiss for me on his "denuded" head and tell him that I would love to see him soon.

Anne

FROM TOP: *Anne at the Cannes Film Festival, 1953 •*
Also at Cannes, with Olivia De Havilland and Shelley Winters

KIRK:

I was going to the Disney studio every day. We usually wrapped midafternoon on Saturday and had Sundays off. That's when I wrote to Anne. I also phoned her and invited her to visit after the Festival was over.

> *Darling—*
>
> *It was nice to get your wire today. I am beginning to like my house more and more. It is really done in good taste and when everything is completely arranged, it'll be even better.*
>
> *I saw Pier and she asked me to take her to the Academy Awards which I am doing, but this is definitely over.*
>
> *I talked with my analyst today and I may go back for more work. The thought depresses me. It's like getting ready to plunge down into some dark, cold and dirty water. It is very difficult getting readjusted to California again,—but it would be much more difficult without a house.*
>
> *Michael and Joel are coming out here this Tuesday for ten days. I'm awfully anxious to see them again. It is their spring vacation.*
>
> *I miss you, Stolz. How is the festival coming along? How long will you be there? And then will you be back in Paris?—*
>
> *Write me again soon because I love to hear from you.*
>
> **Much love, Kirk**

I got this ecstatic response immediately (which meant a week later):

> *My Darling,*
>
> *Have you ever seen anyone so happy in your life? Look at me. It seems to show—everybody tells me that I am en plein sorires [full of smiles]! You cannot imagine at what point of unhappiness and despair I was. I was ready for any stupidity. Then you called me to come for a <u>visit</u>!*
>
> *After your call I went to a party and got tipsy. Nobody understood why. I was celebrating our meeting. I rehearsed what*

I would say to you, then you are taking me in your arms—let's say in a horizontal position? Yes? I cried—I was sooo happy!

Let me talk about you now. Your last letter was written in one of your "Jersey moments."

Darling, I try to understand your situation. So many new feelings and probably people have come into your life since three weeks. Maybe also a few new problems.

But, My Love, do you really think that this necessitates another treatment at your analyst? I don't want to say anything against him. He is certainly a very good doctor and has helped you a lot. Also, I believe that he is even a good friend to you, certainly the most discreet one.

Darling, why don't you talk to him as a friend, go out with him, have lunch and dinner—and don't torture yourself with your past!!! We all have to learn from the mistakes we make in life. Nobody but ourselves can help us! You can make decisions if you have to and you can cope with every problem! So if you have to jump in certain circumstances do it, don't wait until somebody pushes you!! If you hurt yourself, don't worry. It will cure. Let me help you. You know how much you did for me. Let it be my turn sometimes!

The things which are tying us together, most people would not understand. I need you and you might need me a little and, funny enough, this has nothing to do with attraction or sex.—

The Festival is a perfect madhouse with many good pictures. The Academy Award winner will certainly get the Grand Prix. Robert Mitchum (drunk every night and causing a scene with a half-nude French starlet) and Lizabeth Scott (who loves Frenchmen) are replacing Kirk Douglas and Olivia de Havilland from last year. In French we say "grandeur et decadence!" Arlene Dahl and Jack Palance are ignored by the public who don't know them. Gina Lollobrigida has a fantastic success in a picture called Pane Amore e Fantasia *with Vittorio De Sica. Very funny and she is great! You must see it!*

Anne at home in Paris on rue Lord Byron

Directors Preston Sturges and Billy Wilder next week.

The weather is fine, but cold. Get your brain working and make me a long list of everything you want me to bring.

The Festival ends on the 10th and I am leaving for Paris on the 11th. I write to you from there when I will leave. What about your car and your trunk? You must have them by now and all the papers have been shipped a long time ago. I checked on everything before I came down here.

Is there anything you can dream of that you want (aside from me)? Darling, how happy I am. I can't wait anymore. I have no sex life since you left. I am verrrry hungry.

I am sure you are delighted with the kids being there.
I love you. I think of you. I am with you every moment.

Anne (ex-Stolz)

P.S. Let me hear from you again. Your stationery is not
very discreet. Result: Your letter arrived open!

ANNE:

I was dealing with all the complications of Cannes—last-minute requests for tickets, unexpected problems with badly behaved stars, etc. I remember the frantic call I got one night from the Carlton Hotel's concierge: "Robert Mitchum wants us to send up fifteen cases of Champagne!" Of course, the festival would get the bill.

I called Mitchum: "Why do you need fifteen cases of Champagne?"

"I want to take a bath with my naked companion."

I called the concierge: "Send up a few bottles with my compliments. Tell him Madame Buydens suggests you frolic in the bidet."

On March 29, Kirk wrote again. Fran Stark had decorated the San Ysidro house in tones of black and white, and Kirk knew it needed art to make it feel like a real home. Kirk admired my taste and the few pieces I owned. He also trusted my ability to finesse bargain prices. He was sure I could find some wonderful paintings and African sculptures when I was back in Paris. He was a little unrealistic about his expectations for the budget he had in mind, as I soon discovered. I did, however, buy a couple of pre-Columbian statues from the former Mexican jockey, Willie Pierce, I met with John Huston.

My darling Anne—
It was nice to talk to you, but I want to see you. Darling, you
tell me to write anything I feel, but it's very difficult. Often, I
have such strong feelings for you, but I curb myself. I am so
afraid of doing or saying the wrong things in regard to you.
It's funny but I have felt a little mixed up being back here
in California. I saw the analyst and have almost decided to

go again for a while, but it was too difficult because of the children being here.

I will be sending you a check for about six or seven thousand dollars. Put it in my Swiss account. When it is convenient for you, please arrange to come here. Use the money from the checks. Buy first class—not second class accommodations. Fuck Shit Face [Sam Norton]! Nothing but the best for my Stolz.

Also, if you can pick up a few very good paintings reasonably, I wish you would get them—perhaps a Vlaminck, Braque, Utrillo. Also, I understand you can get some wonderful African primitive pieces very reasonably in Paris. You know what I mean—those little black primitive statues of men, etc.—about 10 or 12 inches high. You can spend about $2,000 or so in the paintings if you get something very good at a good price and think you should spend more—go ahead.

I hope all this isn't too much for you to do. If it is, forget it. The more important thing is that you come out here and lie beside me. I hope you like my little house and my very comfortable bed. There is a half of it that has never been used.

You know me, darling, and often I don't say many things that I feel, but always I have a deep wonderful feeling for you—frightening though it may be from time to time.

Please don't work too hard on the festival and let me know when you plan to leave, and more important, arrive. I will put you away in the house for two days to rest up. You are not to see anyone the first day, just sit around the pool and relax until I come home from work.

You'll like the house, I think. I need some paintings—and those African primitive pieces would be wonderful. I miss you, sweetheart—and I'm not stolzig either. Get over here when you can.

Much, much love,
K.

I answered immediately:

Mon Chéri, l'objet de mon adoration!
Ta lettre que j'ai reçu ce matin était tellement gentille et tellement toi que tu m'as faire la plus heureuse de femmes. *[My Darling, the object of my adoration! Your letter that I received this morning was so nice and so you that you have made me the happiest of women.]*

My love—me too, I am afraid of doing the wrong thing—but I don't care. I want to be happy—even if it is only for a short while and you can give me this happiness. I didn't want to say anything about my feelings, not to tell you what is inside of my heart—but I've changed. I don't care anymore, even if you don't like me to say it, if it frightens you. Darling, I love you. And by saying it, I have the feeling that these words have a very poor meaning comparative to the reality.

As soon as I get back I will try to find you the paintings and the African pieces and then I shall put my "little a—" on a plane and when I am in your arms the whole world won't exist anymore for me as long as you want to! You are the boss.

I have changed. I am not at all the Stolz anymore you have known. I have suffered from our separation more than I thought—I miss you so very much. You know that Mr. Lobo might be right. I think I became a virgin for the second time. I can't think of someone else but you touching me.

Darling, I am worried. You tell me that half your bed has never been used? Where on earth are you sleeping every night? Once I am there I will use all your strength and nothing will be left over for an "extra"!!

If you can't write to me here on time, please drop me a note to Paris. I am so happy you are not going back to your analyst. You don't need him anymore. You have everything in yourself which is necessary for your life. Let it come out, speak, decide and act! You can't always be right, but the few times you are will compensate the others!!

It is after midnight. I am terribly tired. Un poete cele-bre français écrivant dans une lettre d'amour à sui maîtresse: Partout on vous voyez du blanc, lisez je vous écrire. *[A famous French poet writing a love letter to his mistress: Everywhere you see white, read what I write you.]*

Anne

KIRK:

My father was getting worse. I flew back to see him in the hospital. I mailed this to Anne on my way to the airport.

Darling—

This evening I am leaving for New York and Albany in order to visit my father. He is still ill and the end is not very far. It was very difficult for me to arrange the visit, but I believe that I must make it. It's a shame you are not with me now. I need you.

I am going to return Sunday because I have to begin work on Monday morning. Enough of sad things—Soon you will be in Paris and you will arrange to leave.

Sam just called me. Monday he is mailing you a check for $7,000—supposedly a loan you gave me during my stay in Paris. Cash it. Use part of it for the paintings if you can find them, the African figures, your expenses—first class—and deposit the remainder in my Swiss account.

Also, Sam asks do you have the papers for the bill of sale for my new car, and the registration papers. I thought I had them, but can't seem to find them.

Now more than ever do I need the love you might hold in your heart for me. To say I miss you seems so inadequate.

Last night I had a little dinner party—Ray and Fran Stark and Merle Oberon. We ran some of the movies I took in Europe and looked at some of the 3D pictures. You are right—I

am so sorry I didn't take more. The pictures at Klosters are
wonderful, but not enough pictures of you.

I have been dating very little—and by the way, did I tell
you . . . I talk too much. I hope you like my little house. It's
simple, but very nice.

Come to me, Darling. My heart is empty and I need
you near. Often I play the French records and I think of us.
Come quickly because my letters are starting to be too long!
I embrace you—

Je t'embrasse *[I embrace you]—Kirk*

ANNE:

Once again, our letters crossed and this lighthearted one of mine was
just simply another report from Cannes:

My darling Ysidor,
I am sitting in the bar waiting for Tola and Arthur Krim
[head of United Artists] *to finish their business before we all*
go over to the "Office" (Casino). I spent a wonderful dinner
with them and both Tola and Arthur have been speaking of
you in such nice terms that it made me suddenly very proud!
Arthur missed you by one day in Jamaica but is looking for-
ward to seeing you in your new house around May 10th.
Tola came down here alone—I am his escort. I really like him
and if it weren't because of you—well—maybe—even though
I know he has the same low character as a man I know who
used to have a beard!

Darling, you can't realize how happy I am that I received
your letters and cable. I don't want to stay on here to rest. As
I told you, I am leaving here on the 11th at night and will
be in Paris on the 12th. I hope to find a letter from you!!!
(Please) and then I try to get your paintings and statuettes
and then—I jump in the first and quickest plane, boat or
bicycle—if necessary, I swim!!

If they make The Racer *in Europe—would you like the idea? Anything can happen these days!!*

Did you try to call me? I had a personal call from New York two days ago and I am still waiting.

Darling, how you miss me! And how I miss you. You can't imagine it.

Anne

I wrote Kirk one final letter (in French) from Cannes at 4:30 in the morning after the Saturday night awarding of the prizes. I was exhausted, but anxious to return to Paris and make my plans for America.

My Darling,
The Gold is over and so is the Festival. Thank God!

Olivia de Havilland made a magnificent speech in French this evening; she received an Oscar from Professor Chrétien [the inventor of CinemaScope]. No one speaks better French in Hollywood than my Ysi! I then decided I am only going to speak French with you. It's not necessary to lose the habit.

I'm leaving for Paris tonight without regret. It's raining terribly here and the weather is frightful. Tola leaves tomorrow. Despite what you think, I have advised him to marry Soph. Tola advised me not to buy paintings without having seen your house. I think he is right.

Kirk—nothing. I just wanted to say your name.

Stolz

KIRK:

Anne and I had spoken by phone and I could hear the weariness in her voice. She said she would stay in New York for a couple of days before coming to me. I knew my Stolz wanted me to see her at her best, so I didn't try to dissuade her. I mailed this letter (written in French, English, and German) to her rue Lord Byron address on April 9, 1954:

Darling,

I received your letter from Cannes. I am going to send this letter to Paris. I am waiting for you patiently—I feel that you are right. It will be much better for you to stay in New York for two days on the way here despite that I miss you and am waiting. If you continue directly here, the trip will be a bit too much for you, I'm sure.

I have missed you very much, Stolz. Everything here has been rather hectic since my arrival—working almost every day, interviews, new house—my kids here for ten days, for which I was very grateful. I don't feel quite here and a little dizzy inside—but always thoughts of you are there.

I try so hard to do the right thing—especially where you are concerned because I love you. I keep thinking I shouldn't have asked you to come here so soon. How ridiculous I can be sometimes. Now I'm so glad you'll be coming out here and I'll take good care of you.

Often I have daydreams about us—while I'm driving home from the studio. I pretend you're waiting for me. We have a drink together, we talk—it's warm, gemütlich. I'm relaxed.

By the way, my butler is Swiss. He speaks French and German as well as English. He's excellent (when he's sober).

My new secretary gives me a pain in the ass—I may not keep her long.

Everyone is so happy that you're coming—Willie, Sam, Ray. Aber mein liebchen kommt. Auch habe ich Peter Lorre gesagst. Er ist sehr interessant deiner Bekanntschaft zu machen—or something like that. [My sweetheart is coming, I also told Peter Lorre. He is very interested in meeting you.]

Darling, when you're not with me, I don't seem to have any desire to show off. I'm learning the banjo to show off some songs for you.

What luck with paintings and African pieces?

Tell me what your plans are: When will you leave Paris? When will you leave N.Y.?

Kirk and new bride pose at home with Pre-Columbian statue

Je t'attendrai ma chérie parce que tu es à moi. *[I'm waiting for you my darling because you are mine.]*

Much, much, you know what!—K.

Anne finalized her departure. She sent me this letter which, unlike most of ours, was headed with the complete date of 14.4.54 (April 14, 1954):

Vous, Mon Impossible Amour,
This is a title of a song—but also you!—J'étais si heureuse avec tes deux lettres et j'adore quand tu parles trop*! I am happy,* incommensuablement *(this is a $3.50 word)* heureuse*!!! [Translation: I was so happy with your two letters and I adore it when you talk so much! I am happy, incommensurably (this is a $3.50 word) happy!!!]*

I am so tired from Cannes. So I've decided to take the boat to New York, the Liberté. I leave April 16 and arrive in New York April 22. It will allow me to rest for six days so that you will see me at my best. I will come Saturday or Sunday, the 24th or the 25th to L.A. I will telephone you and you will tell me which you prefer. I am staying at the Sherry-Netherland in New York.

Darling, I can't think or write anymore. I don't know what to say to you. Open your arms and be nice; I need you so desperately!

Chéri, I hope your father is well again. Please remember whatever happens I am near you under any circumstances!!!

I have been running around for your paintings. I must admit Albert helped me, but frankly, it is a terrible responsibility to choose something of that value. Prices are very high, and I am afraid something more expensive than in America. I also talked to Tola about it. I sincerely feel, Darling, that you have to choose them yourself. It has to be your taste and also one has to know the house even to advise!

Tola gave me permission to see some of his paintings. If there is something you like to have, he will be pleased to let you have them. I think, honestly, that I would rather select them with you on your next trip to Europe in order to avoid a wrong choice.

I have asked for a Duplicate for the bill of sale for your car and will mail same to Sam tomorrow.

Darling, I can't tell you, I look so much forward to talk to you, to see you, to be with you, to love you!!! The idea of waiting for you in the evening when you come home from work—I like!!! And Darling, I won't be STOLZIG anymore. Should I be once or twice please kick me in my little—!

Je suis tellement à toi! *[I am all yours!]*

Anne

CHAPTER FOUR

Together at Last

KIRK:

I went to the airport on April 24, 1954, to meet Anne. Her travel outfit was elegant—a suit that showed her figure to perfection and a chic little hat with a full veil covering her face. I lifted it to kiss her. There were four dark spots of raw skin beginning to crust over.

"My God! What happened?"

"I'd rather not talk about it."

I didn't press her. I took her directly to the house, and we had a beautiful reunion. It was going to be a romantic idyll—nothing permanent, at least not in my mind. Anne had already accepted work on a new film in Paris starring my friend, Marlene Dietrich.

ANNE:

I loved Kirk. I loved the house. I believed when he saw how comfortably I fit into his life in America, he would propose. A month later, I was still waiting for some word about our future.

Kirk had written to me in Cannes about returning to analysis. Now he wanted me to see his analyst, Dr. Kupper, as well. After several sessions, the good doctor advised me to leave Kirk. I was shocked when he also said he had strong feelings for me. I told Kirk; he suggested that maybe Dr. Kupper was the one who should go back into therapy.

All of Kirk's friends—they were now mine as well—expected us to marry. But it looked like I would be going back to my life in Paris, after all.

I wrote Kirk to tell him my plans. It was May 24, exactly a month since my arrival:

My Darling,

In order to put yourself at ease, I write you this note which will avoid any further conversation concerning our relationship.

I decided to leave on the 30th and you have helped me recently to make this decision definite. The reason why I have set this date is familiar to you. Your children are coming out here the 31st and I would not like to lose face in front of them.

But I think I also have to explain to you that the moment I take off from here, I will take you out of my life. I know this won't be easy for me, but I know I will find strength for this somewhere.

In the near future a decision concerning us had to be made one way or the other anyhow. Because, I hate to remind you this, I am a woman—not a little girl—a woman who was capable of deep and sincere love and who knew the real you. I have been completely honest with you and we have known each other well for over one year. I allowed you during this time to push me around emotionally, and if I don't want to get hurt for good, I have to stop you from starting it again.

To face situations once more, of which I had the last example when you left Paris for the Bahamas, and I didn't know whether I would ever see you or hear from you again, no, Kirk, never will I let this happen to me again! I was so miserable and so depressed that I felt no life in me anymore. Remember your answer to this: "Well, I called you, didn't I?" Yes, Darling, you did and I was very happy you invited me out here for a visit.

I know you would not want me to feel that way anymore.

This shows how you can be sometimes wrong in mathematics.

One and one does not always make two. It can also make nothing.—

Let me thank you for the wonderful time you gave me here and for everything else.

Anne

KIRK:

I don't remember responding to Anne. I was working long hours at the studio. A few days later I walked into her room and saw her packing her bags. That's when it hit me. I would be lost without her. Her willpower was much stronger than mine. If she got on that plane, she would never give me another chance.

Suddenly blessed with clarity, I asked Anne to marry me. I would finish filming midday on Saturday, May 29. We could fly to Las Vegas for a license and find a justice of the peace to tie the knot. We'd stay overnight and return to L.A. on Sunday afternoon, so I could get back to work early Monday—the day Michael and Joel would meet Anne again, this time as my wife.

Sam Norton, my publicist Warren Cowan, and their respective wives made up our wedding party. Just as we arrived at the license bureau, it closed for its afternoon break. I started gambling with the boys. Poor Anne stood by fretting at the delay. "I came here to get married," she reminded us.

By early evening, we had the proper papers and Honest John Lytell, J.P. arrived to perform the ceremony. He was a tall Texan, wearing the kind of ten-gallon hat and boots I wore in my westerns.

Before we took our vows, Sam huddled with Anne for a few moments. I paid no attention. It wasn't a romantic wedding, but it was legal. Lytell had a thick drawl which might have challenged even someone born in the U.S. When he intoned, "Do you, Anne, take thee Kirk for your lawful wedded husband?" Anne repeated, "I take thee, Kirk, for my *awful* wedded husband." Everyone laughed and it became our family joke. I thought he meant "full of awe," my bride explained.

ANNE:

I was now Mrs. Kirk Douglas, but even movie stars can't overcome the bureaucracy of two nations— the United States and France. My visa was going to run out in twelve days. I had to return to Paris to apply for new papers as the wife of an American citizen. Neither of us ever dreamed the process would take two frustrating months of separation.

Before I left, Kirk asked again about the facial wounds he saw when I arrived. I took a deep breath and told him: I had crossed the Atlantic by ship only because my former lover insisted I needed the ocean voyage to rest. We had stayed friends and I

Arriving in Las Vegas to get married

was touched at his concern. He even paid the difference between my air fare and the ship passage.

I was feeling pretty good by the time we docked. When I got to the hotel, I was shocked to find my benefactor sitting in the lobby, agitated and clearly intoxicated. He had flown in the night before to surprise me. He was making a scene, so I got him into the elevator and up to his permanent suite. Chain-smoking and belting down more liquor, he begged me not to go to California.

"But I've been in love with Kirk for more than a year," I told him. Hoping to calm him, I said: "If things don't work out, of course I'll come back to you."

In no mood to be reasonable, he ran to an open window and starting climbing through it, swearing he would jump unless I changed my mind. I pulled him away and tried to leave.

FROM TOP: *The morning after—May 30, 1954 • Left to right: The wedding party "on the town"—Ronnie Cowan, Kirk and Anne, Sam and Bea Norton*

This elegant man, whom I had known so well, lunged at me with a lit cigarette. "I'll make sure he doesn't want you," he snarled as he ground it into my face. I was so stunned I didn't feel immediate pain. I telephoned the manager of his New York office to bring a doctor who sedated him and treated my bloody wounds.

Until I could travel, I took refuge with some trusted friends. I wanted to put the whole experience behind me, and I did just that until Kirk brought it up again.

My husband listened to me with compassion. Then he cuddled me in his arms. "I promise, Anne, 'as long as we both shall live,' I will keep you safe." It's been sixty-two years as I write this, and Kirk has always kept his word.

———————┤ ★ ├———————

KIRK:

Anne wrote me from Paris about the vigorous—and sometimes humiliating—vetting she received at the American Embassy. Along with endless forms and proof that she and Albert were legally divorced, she had to endure a complete physical. I was horrified when she described stripping nearly naked and standing in a long line with all the other female applicants. She wanted to do whatever it took to join me, but she drew the line at having a strange gynecologist probe her behind an almost transparent curtain. She insisted on seeing her own doctor.

Anne used the waiting period to settle her affairs. She spent time with her friends and arranged a trip to Hannover to see her sisters. She even went to an art auction in Brussels with her ex-husband, Albert, and bought a small Utrillo for me as a wedding present. She insisted on paying for it with her own money.

I called Anne more often than I wrote. She, of course, resumed her habit of writing me long letters filled with romantic longings and descriptions of her activities. Here is one she wrote on June 21, 1954:

My darling Isidor!

Already complaining, hein *[huh]? I know that you married me for my money but I refuse to spend it on carrier-pigeons so my husband can get my letters in three days!*

*I finally talked to the Consul General today and have sent some more papers to Sam for you to sign. Please have him hurry them back to me, if you still want me—*c'est-à-dire *[that is, to say]! I get nervous and impatient too, Darling, without you. Let's face it. I am not a nice person.*

I found somebody for the rue Lord Byron and a buyer for my car from an ad in the paper. Can we make the gifts to the Nortons and Cowans tax-deductible? If yes, what do you need? A bill, I presume, but for how much?

If you were here (and I wish you were) you would really scream. What you have to go through if you have the craaaazy idea to remarry and if you want to be the only person in this country who would like to do things the way they are prescribed by law, c'est à dire *change your papers, passport, etc. to your new identity. When I come to these 135 different* bureaux, *they all look at me as if to say, Why the hurry?*

Mon chéri, are we really married? I can't realize it. How did I do this? When I look back, I remember I gave myself maybe a 50-50 chance. What happened? Do you think that God felt that I really deserved you and that He wanted to give me the greatest gift you can give a woman—the man she loves with all her heart? Because, my Darling, I really, sincerely have the most wonderful feelings for you and I want so much to make you happy! I have so many more words to tell you this again and again that I hope it will take our lifetime before you get tired of it!

Please take good care. If that visa is not ready when I come back from Germany (I don't know yet the exact date when I am going), I will come back as a tourist and become your mistress!! O.K.? You know that I wake up every morning around 5 a.m. And I can't sleep when I am in bed.

How long can a person live that kind of a no good for nothing life???

I am so pleased that you have been asked to make a recording of "my song" "Whale of a Tale" and even sing it in the picture! Can't you make a little speech before you start to sing, like "This wonderful and thrilling song I dedicate to my awful wedded wife." I should have been in public relations.

I went nightclubbing with George [Cravenne] and Chabert. After dinner we went to Jimmy's, followed by a visit to Elephant Blanc [both popular with the international movie crowd]. Friday I will have dinner with Charles Vanel. He is coming to L.A. for the Hitchcock picture. I gave him your phone no. in case he will be there before I am back.

How is our household? I know you are busy—but write to me as often as you can—I am so happy to get your letters. When Aline brings in my breakfast in the morning, I open one eye to look if there is a letter from you—if not I sleep a bit longer. How I miss you.

Stolz

KIRK:

I was wrapped up in my work. Acting allowed me to lie in bed at night thinking about make-believe people—always so much easier to deal with than real ones.

My father had died shortly before Anne arrived, and I hadn't gone back for his funeral. I still had mixed feelings about him. I received many condolence letters, none more touching to me than the one from my high school teacher, Louise Livingston. I never forgot her important role in shaping my future. She was basically my only remaining tie to Amsterdam and the young dreamer I had been. We stayed in touch for the rest of her life, and I took pleasure in helping her live more comfortably as she aged.

My dear Kirk—

I've been so haunted by your sad happening that I couldn't seem to write at once. Naturally, I've wondered about you and I hope you are passing through the strain of personal affairs and your hard work without a breakdown.

The Times-Union *[Albany newspaper] ran a very fine picture of you with your father and mother. Your devotion will always bring you consolation. Such acts as yours prove a very deep worth. Few people attain greatness. You are well on your way to it.*

Please believe me, Kirk, when I say that I see you HIGHER than all the others. This place you could not achieve without CHARACTER. You possess that, heart and soul. May you be blessed.

It was most wonderful to hear your voice Saturday night. Such a fine talk should bring forth another poem! Of course, I am eager to see you again here, just natural and not in the limelight.

I like this quotation: "Do the Impossible."

I've found that the above comes true. It simply means, Give all you have, work with all your might and hold to <u>Faith.</u>

Do take care of yourself. Keep well and be happy.

As always,
Louise

While Anne was fighting bureaucracy, I was on the backlot at Twentieth Century-Fox making *The Racers*. The main purpose of the film, I soon discovered, was another attempt to make Darryl Zanuck's current mistress a star.

Bayla Wegier was rechristened Bella Darvi by Zanuck and his wife, Virginia Fox, when they discovered her in Monaco. She was a beauty who drank too much and ran up gambling debts she couldn't pay. Her new surname was created from the first syllables of their respective first names: Dar for Darryl and Vi for Virginia. They cleared her debts and brought her to Hollywood.

This film was going to be her third chance at stardom, but she hadn't improved over her first two outings. She eventually went back to France, got fat, gambled compulsively, and committed suicide at age forty-two.

Next I went to Universal to do *Man Without a Star*, a commercial western of no particular artistic merit. I was the producer as well as the star—a new concept in film financing, the fifty-fifty picture. The star got no salary but when the studio recouped its expenses it shared the profits equally. It sounded great to me. But the studio controlled the bookkeeping and the distribution. They made a lot; I made very little, thanks to the creative accounting system that still exists today.

This hardened my resolve to start my own production company. I could ensure my family's financial security and make movies in which I believed. In 1919, Charlie Chaplin, Mary Pickford, Douglas Fairbanks, and D. W. Griffith had banded together to found United Artists for just those reasons.

By 1951, UA had morphed into a financing and distribution company, under the stewardship of Arthur Krim. He helped me a lot when I started Bryna.

Anne and I had been married a month when I got this letter from her.

Sunday, 11:30 p.m.
In bed once more alone!!!

My Darling,
This can't go on—I miss you so much. I am nervous, sad, and impatient. I don't know what to do with myself. I am longing for my awful wedded husband!!!

I am waiting for the papers which I hope Sam has returned. I believe they have been delayed since you were out of town for a couple of days. But I hope to have them here by tomorrow or Tuesday morning at the latest! Then and only then all my papers are filed. If I have the papers by Tuesday, I leave Tuesday afternoon for Bruxelles. There is an auction sale of modern paintings Wednesday. Wednesday night I leave for Hannover, Germany, until Saturday. On Sunday I come back to Paris. So far I have booked a seat on the Parisian Air France for Thursday July 15 provided I have my visa then! I pray to God! The apartment on rue Lord Byron is rented to a very nice man from California. His lawyer takes care of everything (including rent in advance) which will permit me to buy the paintings. My little car is sold too. From tomorrow on I will be without, but when I come back from Germany I will rent one.

I got your letter from Mojave. Is this the only time you go on location for this picture? Why don't you talk about your female co-star [Bella Darvi]. Darling, I am silly but I am so lonely and lost without my husband.

I will ship several paintings and my trunk on a freighter July 21st. We won't have them before end of August. Any other suggestions?

Darling, Saturday night I was married for one month. I refuse to congratulate you because I feel I have been cheated. Now I know why you have so many divorces in America. They don't permit the wives to stay with their husbands! After 12 days—out!! But they don't know STOLZ—as soon as I return I will create the League of the Awful Wedded Wives!!

Chéri, je t'aime, je pense à toi et ne te quitte jamais! [Darling, I love you, I think about you and I will never leave you!]

Stolz

ANNE:

I mailed Kirk this triumphant note from Brussels a few days later:

> **My Darling,**
> The auction was very interesting and the only good buy was the Utrillo pointed out to me by Albert. Guess who bought it? It's an oil painting, 1927 approx., the size of Tola's—$1,500!!!—What a wife you have!
> My darling, now that I know when I am going to you, I can't wait any longer for it. I pray every night for the good God to protect you until my arrival. I'm leaving this evening for Germany. I embrace you my darling with all my heart.
> Stolz

On July 13th, I sent Kirk a cable which read:

> **AM ALL SET NERVOUS AND IMPATIENT PREPARE MY QUARTERS I LOVE YOU=THE IMMIGRANT**

He wired a poetic response immediately:

> **HAVE ALL THE CLOCKS IN THE WORLD STOPPED RUNNING IS THE EARTH NO LONGER REVOLVING ON ITS AXIS LETS GIVE IT A SHOVE=KIRK**

KIRK:

A few days later, Anne was home, all obstacles behind us at last. Now I could turn my attention to setting up my first film, *The Indian Fighter*, under my own banner, the Bryna Company, named after my mother.

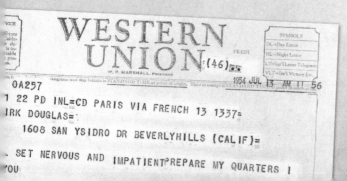

CHAPTER FIVE

Bryna's Early Years

KIRK:

I have always been a maverick; it's worked to my advantage. When producer Hal Wallis signed me for *The Strange Love of Martha Ivers* in 1946, my deal was one picture a year for five years. Later he wanted to give me a more traditional seven-year contract. I said no and he dropped me. Without ties to a studio or a powerful producer, I could decline a role without fear of reprisals. That suited me just fine.

MGM asked me to join *The Great Sinner*—a splashy Technicolor vehicle with a stellar cast: Ava Gardner, Gregory Peck, and Ethel Barrymore. At the same time, an ambitious independent producer named Stanley Kramer wanted me to star in his low-budget, black-and-white film based on a Ring Lardner short story about a boxer named Midge Kelly. I fell in love with Carl Foreman's script. Against my agent's advice, I accepted *Champion*. It made me a bona fide star and earned me my first Oscar nod. As for *The Great Sinner*—a great big flop!

In choosing my first project for Bryna, I once again followed my instincts. *The Indian Fighter* could be a commercial hit if I cast it correctly. I, of course, would star. I wanted Diana—whom we dubbed "Our Ex-Wife"—to be my leading lady. Anne was fine with it.

Normally, she would have gone with me to Oregon, but she was working on a production of her own—our first child. She didn't want to fly or be away from her doctor. The shooting schedule was thirty days, if all went well.

Training for the physically demanding role in Champion *(1949)*

I said to Anne: "Can the boys stay with you while their mother and I are in Oregon?" It may sound odd, but she readily agreed, moving a notch higher on the pedestal I had already built for her.

The script called for a beautiful Indian girl. I was having trouble finding the right actress with the right look. We were at Ray Stark's house one day; Anne and Fran were leafing through *Vogue*.

"This girl would make a fantastic Indian," Anne said excitedly, pointing out a photo of a gorgeous model with high cheekbones coming out of a pool, soaking wet, a man's shirt clinging to her voluptuous body. I finally tracked Elsa Martinelli down through her current beau, Oleg Cassini, who gave me her number. Oleg warned that she spoke terrible English, with a strong Italian accent. No problem, I told him. She'd be eye candy on screen, and who in those prepolitically correct times worried about an authentic accent? My director was André De Toth, a brilliant, half-blind Hungarian whose first of seven marriages was to the *film noir* darling Veronica Lake.

Elsa Martinelli thought it was a joke when I told her I was Kirk Douglas calling to offer her a job. Sing me the song from the Disney picture if it's really you, she demanded in her flawed English. I felt a little silly, but I obligingly crooned a chorus of "Whale of a Tale" to prove it as Anne broke into giggles.

This time Anne and I were in the same country and only one time zone apart. Communication was a lot easier. But we still wrote letters. Anne even wrote me a poem, dated May 24, 1955, about my frenetic preproduction activities. She called it "We Love and Miss You!!!"

> *No more hesitation about firing Cook,*
> *No more doubts about how Martinelli will look.*
> *No more of: "I am lucky to have Andre,"*
> *No more of how they have pushed you at U.A.*
> *No more of: "She would be just right for the part,"*
> *No more questions—to produce you have to be smart.*
> *No more worry about how the weather will be in Bend,*
> *No more kidding, what you need is a helping hand.*
> *No more of "I am so angry at Ray,"*
> *No more of: "Do you love me today?"*
> *No more of our secret luncheon date,*
> *No more: "I have to hurry—I'll be late."*
> *No more. . . . I don't know what to do,*
> *Since more and more I LOVE AND MISS YOU!*
>
> > *Your Baby*
> > *Your Dog*
> > *Your Stolz*

ANNE:

Ironically, Kirk would be with his first wife, not me, on our first anniversary, just five days after I sent him my little poem. His letters to me were loving and enthusiastic about the baby:

Darling—

With all the pens I give out, you'd think I'd have <u>one</u> to write with—but no. We got home early today—about 5.

The kids have left and it feels luxurious to lie in bed here after taking a bath and write to my darling who is getting big with <u>our</u> child and waiting for her husband to come home.

I pray to God that we suddenly don't run into some bad weather. We definitely should finish next week. I hope by Thursday night. If we go until Saturday, that will be exactly thirty days. I hope we can do it under that.

I hope the movie turns out well—I feel sure it <u>can't</u> be something we'll be ashamed of. I hope it will be something we'll be proud of.

I think the kids had a good time here. They wanted to stay, but I think it was best that they go. Yesterday, Joel caught several fish. He was ecstatic. Michael's nose went out of joint. When the two of them are apart, they are great. It's amazing the rivalry between them.

I miss you so much, my darling—no matter how busy I am. And I need you so much. I want our marriage to be a very happy, successful one. I want you to be the way you sound in most of your letters. And I will do everything I can to make it that.

As soon as I finish writing, I'm going to call you on the phone—but it's nice to be able to write a letter sometimes and say things that seem difficult to say on the phone.

My darling, take care of our house, <u>my</u> dog, our baby, and most important yourself. I love you, Stolz—And now I'm waiting for your call to come through. Always remember, darling, I <u>need</u> you—very, very much. And for you, I hope to do some wonderful things in life. This is it—you and me and <u>our family forever!</u>

K.

ANNE:

From the home front, I kept Kirk abreast of my life and what I was hearing when I was out and about with friends. The next movie on Kirk's agenda was *Lust for Life*. He had wanted it to be a Bryna production with Jean Negulesco directing. Stan Margulies, Bryna's head of marketing, announced it in *Variety*. The story got a quick response from MGM. The studio had owned the rights to Irving Stone's book for years; in fact, in 1946 they had planned to make it with Spencer Tracy as Van Gogh.

Kirk was disappointed. Several years earlier Negulesco, a talented artist, had painted Kirk's portrait—adding a beard and a straw hat. His resemblance to Vincent was uncanny. MGM offered him the role in their production, which would reunite him with John Houseman and Vincente Minnelli, the producer and director, respectively, of *The Bad and the Beautiful*. That had been a good experience for Kirk. It earned him a second Oscar nomination. Before he took off for *The Indian Girl* location in Bend, Oregon, Kirk reported to MGM for makeup and costume tests.

I gave my husband some nice news in this letter:

> *My Darling,*
> *Your letters make me so happy, except that they sort of remind me of approximately one year ago. When I was in Paris waiting desperately to hear the "magic" words from you! How foolish can you be! Except that I would make that same damn mistake all over—should you ask me again!*
>
> *Chéri, your two hands won't be big enough to hold one of my "grapefruits"—*
>
> *Dory Schary told Ardy Deutsch that your test in Van Gogh's makeup is sensational! Darling, I wish you all the luck in the world—take it easy—don't make up for the others!*
> ***I miss you terribly—Stolz***

KIRK:

The picture was coming in on schedule, and I was eager to go home. Whenever I was away, I always tried to call Anne on Sunday, the only day we didn't work as a rule. I tended to write her as well, just before or after our conversations.

Darling—

Here it's Sunday—the day of rest—and I've been out for most of it shooting publicity pictures.

We are hoping to finish the picture by Thursday night, but the assistants feel it will take until Friday. I hope I'll be home Friday with my darling.

This morning we went over the rest of the stuff that must be shot with Andre and Willie [Schorr]. We should have no problems and the rest of the stuff should be rather simple to shoot. Let's pray that the weather holds up!

Willie just called to ask me to join him and Andre for a beer, but I feel so lazy. I think I'll just stay here and write to you and wait for my call to you to go through.

It was very nice of you to let Diana stay at the house. Michael told me so, too, when I talked to him yesterday.

I haven't even had a chance to read any of the books that I brought with me on Van Gogh. But there'll be time enough for that—I just want to lie around the pool and take life easy.

The Sunday Breakfast was a great success—we all loved it!—And with it, we ate one of the trout that Joel caught.

Just talked with you on the phone—will be talking to you again tomorrow. Very excited about the baby moving! You sound so happy, but remember—community property—she's or he's half mine!

All my love, Kirk

As soon as I was back in Beverly Hills, MGM called me in to sign a loyalty oath. I objected vehemently to the practice. The studios required it, not because they questioned our loyalty but in order to appease the House Un-American Activities Committee (HUAC). I had to sign if I wanted to play Vincent.

The "Red Scare" had become embedded in the collective national conscience some eight years earlier, thanks to the all-powerful HUAC, which focused on the movie industry primarily so they could get front-page publicity.

The top brass of the studios and distribution houses got together at the Waldorf-Astoria Hotel in November of 1947 to discuss how they could defuse the impression they were riddled with "Commies" and "Pinkos." They created the infamous blacklist, which destroyed the lives of so many talented people. Ironically, while all this was going on, the Communist Party itself was never outlawed.

As far as I was concerned, the Committee's methods were un-American, but I signed the oath. I was ashamed to do it. The memory of how I felt spurred me to hire blacklisted writers such as Dalton Trumbo for my own company, using the elaborate system of fake names they created. Dalton's was Sam Jackson.

The achievement I am proudest of in my long life is helping to break the blacklist by using Dalton's given name in the credits of *Spartacus*. But before that could happen, I would be adding to my filmography with *Lust for Life*, *Gunfight at the O.K. Corral*, *Paths of Glory*, *The Vikings*, and *The Devil's Disciple*.

ANNE:

Lust for Life was going to shoot on locations in Belgium, Holland, and France—all the actual places where Van Gogh lived. In Arles, Kirk slept in Vincent's room in the inn where he died. I was excited to be returning to Europe with Kirk.

I wasn't with him for the arduous locations in Holland. He wanted me to remain in Paris with friends. I didn't know whether we could see each other before I went back to California to await our child. Luckily, the production would move back to the MGM backlot and Kirk would be home when Peter Vincent Douglas was born, on November 23, 1955.

Here's what Kirk wrote me in Paris before I left.

Darling—

I am going to call you later today to find out whether or not you will be leaving tonight. There is a chance we might finish tomorrow, but we still don't know. They may cut out a scene here. The letter that you wrote to Amsterdam finally arrived today. It was a sweet letter!—

How do you feel back home in our house? How was the trip? It seems strange to be asking about things before they happen. I want you to take very good care of yourself—sit around the pool—with the phone by your side.

I wonder if they are certain now about the release date of Indian Fighter. *Stan [Margulies] says it might be right after Xmas.*

The weather here has been cold and damp. I bought a pair of wool-lined shoes and a sweater. On the whole, I think the picture is going well. But I've had it, and I'm ready to go back. Now that you are leaving, I don't look forward to going back to Belgium. I wanna go home.

This castle [the hotel Kasteel Maurick in Rotterdam] seemed like a dream place at first. Now it seems cold and dreary.

I'm glad I had a chance to visit the museums in Amsterdam— even though I had to do it quickly. The collection of Van Goghs is fantastic—not to mention the Rembrandts, Hals, Vermeer.

I'm almost tempted to call you and tell you not to leave Paris this weekend in the hope that I might be able to get there!—I'm writing this on location with many interruptions—it's been raining from time to time.

I better end this. I've already talked to you on the phone and we are going to try to meet in Paris this weekend.

All my love, K

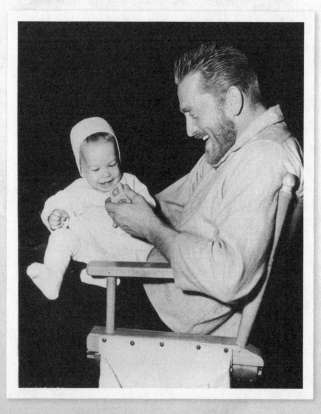

FROM TOP: *At home with baby Peter • Peter visits daddy on the set of Lust for Life (1956)*

KIRK:

Lust for Life took a toll on my psyche. As an actor, I knew how to create an illusion without getting lost in the role. Until Vincent. I was exactly his age at his death. I looked so much like his self-portraits that people gasped when I stood in front of one in the museum. I could feel the tortured artist taking over my soul.

Part of my transformation into Van Gogh was wearing heavy work shoes like his. I always kept one untied so that I would feel unkempt, off balance, in danger of tripping. I walked with a shuffling gait. I continued to wear them for months after the movie

Peter sees the world from on high

was done. I swear I would sometimes check my ear to make sure it was there! I felt haunted, but Anne and the happiness we felt about our baby broke the spell.

The Indian Fighter was doing respectable business, and now I needed to decide on Bryna's next projects. I started going to the office every day. I read books and scripts and went to a great many bullshit meetings.

I was just getting used to this routine when Anne reminded me she still had to fulfill her contract to handle protocol for one more Cannes Film Festival. It was April 1956, exactly two years, one marriage, and one baby since her last tour of duty. Peter was five months old.

We were back to exchanging letters. Here's what Anne wrote me at midnight on the first of May. She refers to the Picasso vase that sits in the entry foyer of our house, encased in Plexiglas. Anne had it appraised recently by Sotheby's. They set its current value at one million dollars.

My Darling,

I am so sad and depressed—I don't think I ever wanted to be near you as much as right now.

The toilet paper is too hard, the coffee is too strong, the water has an awful taste, the telephones are impossible. Don't I sound like a true American? But even being a European broad, what on earth am I doing here!!!

The Festival—my God—I couldn't care less. I have never had such a wonderful and inexpensive vacation. But who needs it when you have a little son waiting for you?

Daryl Zanuck and Bella are back together, closer than ever. Bella has the most gorgeous diamond necklace I have ever seen. She also won five million francs last night at the Casino. The night before her departure for Rome, Kim Novak was in a serious flirtation with Aly Khan. Harry Cohn might have a heart attack if he gets his second big star involved with this Arabian Prince. So go the gossips.

I went yesterday to Vallauris, buying posters for us and Dr. Kupper. I also was so enchanted with one of Picasso's latest pottery—a big vase—that I bought it. It will be sent directly. Cost me only $200. It is for our new house and I am sure you will love it.

Everybody from MGM told me that at their last great convention they saw Lust for Life which they consider as the greatest picture done after the war. Also they are prepared to give for this picture the greatest publicity buildup with charity opening at the Paris Opera for reconstruction and simultaneous openings in three key European cities. They would very much like for you to come. It will be sometime between the 1st–15th of October. By "they" I mean Metro Europe.

Never mind all the dinners you have with Michael and Joel—how about the dinner with Mary Preminger? Don't think I have my information from Otto. [Preminger was a member of the Cannes Jury.] I told him, and boy, did we fix you. We immediately lunched together the next day. But—didn't you tell me once that Mary would be your cup of tea? How many cups did you have?

It is misery without you and my little Peter. I take one look at his pictures and I cry like an idiot. Do you realize what he really means to me? Let's have another one.

Darling, we are so happy and give each other so much and I need you deeply. I love you. That you must believe because it is true.

Stolz

CHAPTER SIX

1957: On Location in Arizona, Germany, and Norway

KIRK:

Nineteen fifty-seven started with me in Tucson for *Gunfight at the O.K. Corral*. I was Doc Holliday and Burt Lancaster was Wyatt Earp. I hadn't worked with "Boit" since *I Walk Alone*, ten years earlier. We never seemed to run out of things to say to each other—much of it the kind of ribbing that good friends who are also highly competitive enjoy.

Burt had formed his production company, Hecht-Hill-Lancaster, shortly before I set up Bryna. We both knew the studio system was rigged against us; we wanted the freedom to choose our projects—whether or not they were deemed commercial.

Burt was still working off the seven-year contract he had with Hal Wallis—the one I had turned down years before. I convinced him to take the role in *Gunfight*; it would be his final piece of indenture. As a free agent, I was in a great bargaining position with Hal. Bogart had rejected the part, and preproduction had already begun. I got ten times what I would have received if I were still under contract, and double what Burt was making.

That would help pay the bills, because my next movie—*Paths of Glory*—was definitely not going to be a moneymaker.

This would be my first of two experiences with Stanley Kubrick, whom I have described over the years as "a talented shit." I had contacted the young filmmaker after seeing his low-budget movie *The Killing*. I asked if he had any other projects, and he gave me the script for *Paths of Glory*. Stanley had adapted a 1935 novel about corruption and greed in the high command of France during World War I into a brilliant screenplay. He had been peddling it around Hollywood with no success.

I already had a deal with Arthur Krim of United Artists to finance *The Vikings*. I convinced him to give me a budget of $1.25 million to make *Paths of Glory* while we were setting up my "Norse opera." We shot in and around Munich, using castles that looked French and fields where we could reproduce battle scenes.

Our home base in Munich was the Geiselgasteig Studios. The war had destroyed this once-thriving operation. Ironically, it took two American Jews, Douglas and Kubrick, to breathe new life into the dilapidated studio and the local economy. The studio was very close to Dachau, the notorious concentration camp.

My first fight with Stanley and his partner, James Harris, was over the script. I loved the one I saw in Los Angeles, even though I was frank about its lack of commercial appeal. In a misguided effort to remedy that, Stanley had rewritten it. It was terrible.

In the new version, my character, Colonel Dax, said stupid things. At the end, he goes off with the general he had bitterly opposed to have a drink. I threatened Stanley: "We will make the script I bought or we won't make the film at all." Stanley nodded silently, and we went to work.

Kubrick and I had a three-picture deal. After *Paths of Glory*, I was happy to honor his request to release him from our agreement. It amused me years later when Stanley told people I was only an employee on the movie. I have a healthy ego, but his was gigantic.

It was a lonely shoot, with Anne and little Peter back in Beverly Hills. Here's what I wrote her on March 14, 1957:

Darling—

How is it that when I am away from you, such love for you overwhelms me that at 2:30 in the morning—as it is now—I awake to write to you.

Suddenly I look at your picture and my need for you and Peter is overpowering. How incomplete I seem without my family. How can any man live alone? To live just for yourself is to be dead. And yet I welcome this parting from you to rekindle my awareness of how much you mean to me.

The early hour brings out the poetic side of me.

By the way, Frances Goldwyn told me that her opinion of me went much higher when I married you! So many compliments for you. You'll be spoiled!

So much for now—Goodnight to you & Peter.

K.

I was delighted when Anne decided to bring Peter to Munich to see Daddy, but first I needed to update her on *The Vikings*.

Darling—

It was nice to talk to you on the phone. I miss you and Peter very much. I'm so happy that you will both be coming soon.

After I talked with you, Arthur Krim called me. He says that Tony Curtis wants to play Eric and Janet Leigh will play the girl. At first I thought: gosh, no, but I told him I'd think about it. I feel it may be the solution. He's not ideal for the part, but he's younger than I and with a little rewriting I could make Hasting [Einar in the final script] a good part for me to play and try to make a big commercial box-office hit out of the picture. The cast would begin to look big—

Kirk Douglas, Tony Curtis, Ernest Borgnine, Janet Leigh, Michael Rennie, Etc.

What do you think? Krim is all for it. This may be the solution. I'll sleep on it.

I'm so tired tonight & so anxious to have you & Peter here with me.

All my love to both of you——K.

ANNE:

Kirk knew that I saw things from a business standpoint more than a strictly creative one. It made me feel much closer to him when he asked what I thought. I never hesitated to tell him, but I always made it clear I deferred to his judgment. I replied to his letter immediately:

Mon Liebling,

I surely don't agree with Tony as a Viking—but who cares if he is box office and you can get a better deal. He is just like a kid. What a pity to give up your part of Eric. I thought that you and Van Heflin would be much better—but, again, who am I—I'm nothing!

I got bad news from Paris. They expelled me from the apartment. I don't know how this happened—why nobody informed me about it! Well, that is tough luck!

Last night I went to the Vidors and saw the Wilders. I showed Billy all the clippings from your arrival in Germany. He was very pleased. Tony Curtis and Janet Leigh were there. (He told me they would <u>consider</u> to go to Norway!) Well, we'll see.

I had my second typhoid shot and feel lousy again—but you know tomorrow I will be O.K. Oh, by the way, we got the other Palm Springs house—$68,000 including the maid's room! Not bad! They consider this the best deal ever made for anybody. But now we have two houses in Palm Springs! The other one should go up for sale immediately, but Sam

[Norton] wants to have it rented just for six months—but try to explain to Sam that nobody wants to rent a house in Palm Springs between June and October!!

Darling, I feel so lonely without you. I wish you were with me right now. I love you very much.

Stolz

KIRK:

I was still in Munich the night of the Academy Awards. I was nominated—my third time—for playing Vincent van Gogh. According to Mike Todd and all my other Hollywood pals, I was the odds-on favorite to win. On Oscar night, I was a continent away from the ceremonies. There was a gaggle of journalists and photographers camped out overnight in the lobby of Hotel Vier Jahreszeiten [*the Four Seasons*] to get my reaction to my victory. I sent Anne this cable before I went to bed:

NO MATTER WHAT I STILL HAVE TWO OSCARS YOU AND PETER ALL MY LOVE=KIRK

I lost to Yul Brynner in *The King and I.* The media went away. I stayed in my room. Anyone who says they don't care about winning is lying. It hurt.

While I was still brooding, the bellman delivered a package. The desk had orders from my wife to deliver it only if the prize eluded me once again. I opened it. Inside was a golden facsimile engraved "To Daddy who rates an Oscar with us always. Stolz and Peter." It is one of my most precious possessions.

In 1996, when I received my Oscar for Lifetime Achievement, I fulfilled a promise I made to myself in Munich thirty-nine years before. If I ever got the real thing, I would give it to Anne. But on March 27, 1957, I could only give her this cable:

BELIEVE ME DARLING NO OTHER AWARD COULD MEAN AS MUCH TO ME AS THE OSCAR YOU AND PETER SENT ME ALL MY LOVE=KIRK

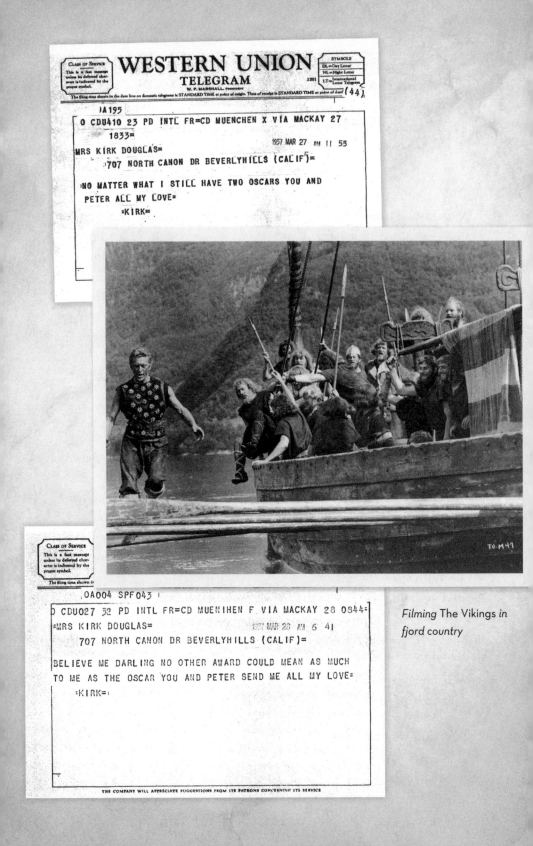

WESTERN UNION TELEGRAM

W. P. MARSHALL, President

1201

(44)

The filing time shown in the date line on domestic telegrams is STANDARD TIME at point of origin. Time of receipt is STANDARD TIME at point of destination

JA195

O CDU410 23 PD INTL FR=CD MUENCHEN X VIA MACKAY 27

1833=

MRS KIRK DOUGLAS=   1957 MAR 27 AM 11 55

707 NORTH CANON DR BEVERLYHILLS (CALIF)=

NO MATTER WHAT I STILL HAVE TWO OSCARS YOU AND

PETER ALL MY LOVE=

=KIRK=

OA004 SPF043

O CDU027 32 PD INTL FR=CD MUENCHEN F VIA MACKAY 28 0844=

=MRS KIRK DOUGLAS=   1957 MAR 28 AM 6 41

707 NORTH CANON DR BEVERLYHILLS (CALIF)=

BELIEVE ME DARLING NO OTHER AWARD COULD MEAN AS MUCH

TO ME AS THE OSCAR YOU AND PETER SEND ME ALL MY LOVE=

=KIRK=

Filming The Vikings *in fjord country*

ANNE:

On Oscar night I was in the audience with Willie Wyler. When Tony Quinn walked off with Best Supporting Actor for playing Paul Gauguin in *Lust for Life*, my hopes rose. It was a hard night for me. Kirk wouldn't hear the news until many hours later. I wrote him the next day:

> *My Darling,*
>
> *This is not a letter of consolation. I feel and I always felt that you should have won—but things are not always the way they should be, so I feel we must be happy with what we have—and we have plenty. I am extremely happy with you and I hope you are too. We have our Peter in good health—beautiful houses, money in banks all over the world—is there anything more we can ask?*
>
> *The show was quite an experience for me! I hated every minute of it. Afterwards, Willie Wyler and I went to the Vidors—thirty people had bets on you, everyone but Martin Gabel. Everybody was disappointed. But you too have now your Oscar to put on your mantel. I bet you never thought your old lady would be so clever!*
>
> *How I love you, my Darling. Suddenly I would love to be alone with you somewhere. Please, my love, let us concentrate on us a little bit more—it would help our relationship tremendously. Also let us talk together a bit of your future business plans. Why do you want to compete? Make an occasional picture for your company, with a producer-director of your choice. You do not need a big organization.*
>
> *I met Maria Schell tonight and she wants us to come to her house in Munich.*
>
> *I love you so much and I want you close to me. Just you and me.* Ich liebe dich.
>
> *Stolz*

Kirk with his "Oscar" from Peter and Anne

KIRK:

The picture was moving along on schedule. I had a day off and decided to go to Dachau, which was open to the public, its grass growing on soil fertilized by the dead. I went into the shower rooms where so many Jews had breathed in lethal gas and into the crematoria, where their bodies were turned into ash. Of course, it had all been sanitized and down-played for visitors.

None of the Germans we met during our stay admitted to knowing what went on at Dachau. But there must have been a perpetual cloud of noxious smoke blowing over their homes. I had immersed myself in a film about the insanity and brutality of war, so I was even more sensitive to the horrors of the more recent conflict.

Stanley cast his future wife, Christiane Harlan, as the German cabaret singer. I discovered that she was related to the Nazi filmmaker Veit Harlan, who had directed the virulent anti-Semitic propaganda film, *Jud Suss* (Suss the Jew). I hoped her relative was gnashing his teeth in hell to know his "pure" blood was mingling with *Jud Kubrick*.

After we wrapped the production, I left for Norway to start work on *The Vikings*. That proved to be an arduous shoot in inhospitable locations, fraught with unforeseen delays. Except for Tony and Janet, none of us were with our families. I was doing my best not to grumble, even though I had to insert a painful prosthetic shield over one eye each day.

Tony described in his 1993 autobiography how he and I huddled under a lean-to tarp waiting for the rain to stop (it never did) "shivering, miserable, thirty-five days behind schedule, hundreds standing around, money going down the drain." He recalled my looking at him and asking, "Tony, do you want to buy a company cheap?"

When our Norwegian longboat crews threatened to quit unless I raised their salaries, I blew up. I had treated them like comrades-in-arms and they were trying to take advantage of me. We pared the rest of the location shots and wrapped, leaving behind the stunned Norwegians—now suddenly eager to go back to work at their old salaries.

Getting out of fjord country and its perpetual rain certainly lightened my spirits. Back at the Munich studio, things went more smoothly on *The Vikings*. Anne and Peter had visited for a few weeks, so I was more optimistic than I had been in Norway.

I scheduled a premiere of *Paths of Glory* for September 18, 1957, in Munich—the first one in the history of the city. It had opened in America to dismal box office. The reviews, however, were glowing. Hollis Alpert of *The Saturday Review* said it was "unquestionably the finest American film of the year . . . so searing in its intensity that it will probably take its place in years to come as one of the screen's most extraordinary achievements."

It certainly helped establish Kubrick as an important filmmaker. Difficult as he was, there was no question about his extraordinary talent. That's why I was willing to put up with his less attractive qualities when I hired him for *Spartacus* a couple of years later. The Munich premiere was a big success; I wrote Anne about it the next day:

Darling,

How dreary Munich is without you and Peter!—

I went through the entire picture [The Vikings] yesterday and I think it's quite good. We are making many cuts and revisions. The picture should run about 2 hrs.

Billy Wilder and Tola Litvak were here yesterday but I saw them very briefly. Frankly, I was miffed that they didn't come over to the theatre to see Paths of Glory *even for a short time to take some pictures with me.*

I made a speech in German at the theatre—big hit. The movie has gotten good notices but is only doing fair-good business. Apparently the theme is much too strong for the women and also makes the Germans a little uncomfortable.

God, how I miss you and Peter. Last night, at the studio Elmo Williams' [second unit director] baby ran to him yelling "Daddy." Was I jealous!

I keep telling myself that I'm working for us and that keeps me going. I may have several days off next week while they are putting together the changes. Maybe I'll go to Paris—look at some paintings, etc. Anything you want me to do for you?

(I've just noticed that on the other side of this page are some notes while I was working out my speech!)

Darling, I love you and Peter more than you will ever know—And I need you both.

Please take good care of yourself and I'll write again soon.

All my love—K.

ANNE:

I was very fond of both Anatole Litvak and Billy Wilder. I tried to calm Kirk down:

Dear Daddy,

I don't know where you are—but wherever—I love you. I got two letters from you today. Don't be angry with Billy and Tola. They are the greatest egos and egocentrics anyway and only Dr. Kupper could probably help them. Then again their egos would not permit it.—

When are you coming home? Willie [Schorr] and his bride have come down for two days. She is very nice and they seem to be very happy.

Come home. I need you so terribly and miss you like mad. Peter wants his daddy too and I want my man.

Stolz

KIRK:

I treated myself to those few days in Paris. I added to our art collection while I was there, but staying in the city I loved without Anne was torture. I wrote her this on September 23, 1957:

Darling—

It's 8 in the morning but I thought I would write you a few lines before going to the studio. Aren't you glad you're not with me now—stirring around so early in the morning?? We've got to work out many things—including fixing up my room so that all I have to do is quietly go in there when I want to wake up early.

I'm so anxious to get back and take things easy. You must help me. I want to really relax and work out lots of little annoying things. I want to be able to arrange my life so that I will work at peace when I'm working—have a quiet place to study—and live happily with my family at other times.

Last night I came back from Paris and Jerry [Vikings line producer Jerry Bresler] and I had dinner with Nascimbene, the composer. We had a drink and we all agreed on one thing—that it is terrible for a man not to be married. Nascimbene felt a man in the artistic field did much better when he was married. Here we were—three men—who each admitted they were very much in love with their wives. Surely, it comes as no surprise to you that I love you very much—you and Peter—and that I miss you very much.

I went crazy in Paris—bought paintings like mad:

1 Vlaminck [a Fauve master of the early 1900s]— $12,000, bargained from $15,000

1 Vlaminck—$10,000

2 Fass $1,000—you will love these paintings and I think this guy is really something.

About eight other paintings which may become something—but inexpensive.

I feel now with our Vlaminck flowers, we have a nice collection of Vlamincks. Next we'll get something else—possibly a real good painting that we'll donate to a museum.

Izzy—the collector of rags, bones, bottles and paintings— is on his way!

I love you—but please take good care of yourself and keep in constant check with the doctor—maybe you should have another one as well! Kiss Peter for me.

K.

CHAPTER SEVEN

Facing Difficulties at Home

KIRK:

I couldn't wait to get back to Anne and Peter after production on *The Vikings* wrapped. While I was still abroad, Anne told me I was going to be a father again, sometime in June of 1958. I had been imagining an idyllic respite with my family. Unfortunately, far from enjoying unbroken domestic bliss, Anne and I were at loggerheads about Sam Norton—my best friend, lawyer, and business manager for almost fifteen years. To be honest, Sam gave me the love and attention I never experienced with my father. I trusted him completely.

Anne was not a fan, and Sam did little to woo her. While I was in Munich, Anne had written me a letter in which she described how Sam had disrespected her. It read in part:

> *For a change I got really mad at Sam today. He announced to me* en passant *that he rented the Palm Springs house to Gordon MacRae for one month for $1,250—we to pay gardener and pool. I just asked why I was not consulted and he said that this is business which did not concern me and I should stick to what to buy at Saks or Magnin's! Can you imagine*

me—it was ten times worse! After I told him very calmly that he was insulting my intelligence, I also advised him to speak to the Gregory Pecks, who had expressed the wish to take the house for the season with an option to buy. He also calmed down and invited me for lunch tomorrow.

During her visit to Munich with Peter, Anne had seen the note Sam sent me—no sugar-coating—to say *Spring Reunion* was a box-office flop. Sam had insisted that, for tax purposes, Bryna needed to produce movies I didn't star in. I didn't like the idea; but, as usual, I followed his advice. Another production, *Lizzie*, had also lost money. Sam's news depressed me.

I didn't know about this letter Anne wrote. I can see how hard she tried, for my sake, to be diplomatic:

Dear Sam:

I hope you don't mind my writing you this personal letter, but since I'm most concerned about Kirk's health I feel it is imperative. I do not know if you realize in what state Kirk is actually. Overworked and exhausted. Therefore your letter—I mean your two lines—of yesterday, with which you forwarded to him Myer Beck's statement on Spring Reunion *was a terrible blow to him. I don't mean only the actual figures, Sam, but I do also mean the way you brought this to his attention. I feel very strongly that one cannot bring such a news to a client, and even less to a friend, in just two lines without any comments on your behalf. I'm surprised that your psychologic knowledge didn't tell you that you had to explain this a little more detailed rather than merely forward the message.*

Sam, I do hope that you understand my note to you in the right way; I don't think I would have written it unless I personally would have felt so strongly about it, and if I wouldn't have been so worried about Kirk.

All the best to you and Bea.

Love, Anne

ANNE:

My suspicions about Sam continued to build. I certainly didn't believe my husband was as financially secure as Sam proclaimed. There was no paperwork to back up his repeated assurance that Kirk was a millionaire. Meanwhile, the play, *A Very Special Baby*, for which Kirk guaranteed the financing, closed after a one-week run on Broadway—another result of Sam's advice to diversify.

Some of our friends tried to tell Kirk to rescind Sam's power of attorney. It wasn't wise to give another person so much control over one's earnings, they said. But Kirk always brushed their doubts aside. He supported Sam all the way—in more ways than he could possibly have imagined, considering what I learned after investigation.

Our most contentious fight happened when I told Kirk what Sam had done to me in Las Vegas just before we were married. He handed me a legal document and a pen and told me to sign. I had no time to read it. This went against everything my father had taught me, but *stolzig* just then was out of the question. The justice of the peace was ready to join me to the love of my life. After only a few days of marriage, I had to return to Paris to go through the excruciating two-month process of getting my American papers. I was dependent on Sam to help me through the legalities. But now, nearly two years later, I wanted to read what I had signed on May 29, 1954.

"Don't worry, Anne," Sam said. "It's just a prenup. Everyone in America has one." He brushed off my request for a copy.

KIRK:

I didn't know we had a prenuptial agreement. I only knew that, like always, Sam had my best interests at heart. I refused to get in the middle of it.

Anne saw she was fighting a losing battle. She dropped the subject. I underestimated my wife. Without telling me, she hired Greg Bautzer, one of Los Angeles's most prominent attorneys, to sue Sam for a copy. Once Bautzer had it, Anne and he pored over it together.

Our discord resumed: "Did you know," Anne demanded, "that I and *my* children have no claim on your estate until we're married five years?

What if, God forbid, something happens to you—if one of your danger-ous stunts, like walking the oars on that Viking ship, were to go terribly wrong? How would I provide for Peter and the new baby? Where would your money go? To Sam, no doubt, using his power of attorney."

I was angry, not at Sam but at my wife. Sam prepared a document giv-ing Anne ownership of all our art, some of which she had brought with her into our marriage. This, he assured me, would satisfy her.

This only fed the flames of her indignation. Anne's lawyer prepared a new will for me and Anne insisted I take out a very expensive insur-ance policy. If only to restore my happy home life, I agreed to both.

I took refuge from these domestic upsets in work. I read Howard Fast's book, *Spartacus*, at the suggestion of Eddie Lewis, a talented producer I had under contract. I optioned it from Howard. I joined forces with Burt and his company for *The Devil's Disciple*, an adaption of the George Bernard Shaw play, to film in London. I wouldn't have any of the actual producing headaches on this one, but would share in the profits.

Sir Laurence Olivier—arguably the greatest actor alive—wanted to be in it. Perfect! I could ask him to direct *Spartacus* when we were in England. Hopefully, I would have a good enough script by then to interest my dream cast of British stars: Olivier, Charles Laughton, and Peter Ustinov.

My good spirits returned. United Artists was pleased with what they were seeing of *The Vikings* in postproduction. I was looking forward to working with Burt again and putting together *Spartacus*. Anne and I were spending long weekends at our Palm Springs house, where my pal Mike Todd and Elizabeth Taylor lived across the street from us.

ANNE:

I had never seen Mike as besotted with any woman as he was with Eliza-beth. Here's one of my favorite memories. On a weekend break from *The Vikings*, Kirk and I went to see them in London at the Dorchester Hotel. Elizabeth was pregnant with Liza, who would be born on August 6, 1957.

When we arrived at their suite, Elizabeth was in bed eating choco-lates. Mike poured us some drinks. Elizabeth kept calling to Mike for more treats. Finally he went into the bedroom and yelled, "Just shut up and be beautiful!"

A bit later, Mike said, "Let's have dinner." He went back to Elizabeth. "What would *you* like to eat tonight, sweetheart?"

It was about seven o'clock by then. Kirk and I were giggling as we listened to their conversation:

"Mike, do you remember that little French restaurant on the Left Bank in Paris where we had that delicious meal a week ago?"

"Yeah, I remember."

"I feel like that."

Mike got on the phone to the restaurant. He chartered a plane, had the food put aboard, and sent a car and driver to fetch it from the aircraft as soon as it landed. We ate that dinner at 10 o'clock. Now that's a showman!

KIRK:

Mike was a fantastic guy, but I hoped his extravagance with Elizabeth wouldn't give Anne ideas!

In Palm Springs on Friday, March 21, 1958, Mike phoned us to come over and see his latest gesture of love. Spread atop the grass was an extraordinary array of jewels: necklaces, bracelets, rings, earrings—all encrusted with precious stones and shimmering like a mirage in the late-morning sun. Mike had gotten Van Cleef & Arpels to set up the display before Elizabeth woke up. Then he led her out to it and said, "Go ahead. Pick whatever you want." It wasn't her birthday; it wasn't their anniversary; it wasn't a holiday. Mike didn't need a reason to indulge his passion for his young wife.

The following morning, March 22, I was on Mike's tennis court for our regular game. "You sure know how to make a guy look bad with his wife," I joshed him about the jewels.

Mike was flying to New York later that day with a few pals. Elizabeth wouldn't be going. She had a cold. "Come with us," Mike urged. "You can present me with the award I'm getting and then, tomorrow, we can stop in Independence, Missouri, and visit with Harry Truman."

Truman was an idol of mine. It sounded like a lot of fun. I went home to tell Anne.

ANNE:

I was six months pregnant, and this time together with Kirk was very precious to me. Soon he would be promoting *The Vikings* and then leaving for England to make *The Devil's Disciple*.

Kirk came back from the match in high spirits. "Guess what, darling, I'm flying to New York with Mike in a few hours."

I don't know what came over me, but I had a strange feeling. "Absolutely not, Kirk. I don't

Surviving Mike—Elizabeth and Kirk dance at Spartacus *premiere*

want you on that plane. You can fly commercial and meet him there."

We started to fight. "I'm expecting a child and you know I don't want you to go," I insisted. Kirk gave in. He was furious. If he couldn't fly with Mike, he wouldn't go at all. I was ruining his fun for no logical reason. He stomped off to bed without kissing me goodnight.

KIRK:

In the morning we piled into the car—Peter, his nanny, Anne and me. We still weren't talking as we headed toward L.A. To break the uncomfortable silence, I turned on the radio. Within minutes the music was interrupted by a news flash. Mike's plane, the *Lucky Liz*, had crashed over New Mexico a few hours after takeoff. No survivors.

I pulled onto the shoulder of the road immediately. Shakily, I got out of the car. Anne joined me. We stood, wrapped together in a strong embrace, tears streaming down our faces. Finally I said, "Darling, you saved my life. I will always trust your intuition from now on."

Just one year into their marriage and the happiest I'd ever seen her, Elizabeth Taylor was a widow at twenty-six. Eddie Fisher, Mike's best friend, stepped in to console her—and we all know where that led. I wonder who of my friends would have stepped in with Anne?

Maybe I was channeling Mike when I planned the publicity and marketing campaign for *The Vikings*. He was the greatest showman of our times.

Arthur Krim had been patient with me during filming, which went a million dollars over the initial budget. I had strived to make the picture historically accurate. We built an entire Viking town. We paid Norwegian rowing clubs to be the oarsmen on Viking ships, constructed to the dimensions of the ninth-century originals. I even lived aboard one of them with some of the cast to get the feel of being Viking.

Before the film opened, we sent Viking dagger letter openers to members of the press. For the May 9 premiere in New York, seven Viking vessels, en route from Bergen, Norway, would arrive to great fanfare in New York harbor.

We had a 261-foot replica of a Norse ship hoisted above the marquee of the Victoria and Astor Theatres at Broadway and Forty-Fifth Street—several stories high and almost a block long. I was hauled up in a boatswain's chair and christened the prow with a bottle of champagne. Then Tony, Janet, Ernie, and I waved from the boat to the crowd below.

Anne was too far along in her pregnancy to be there, but I brought my mother down from her Albany nursing home. She saw her name in lights over Times Square: "BRYNA PRESENTS THE VIKINGS." She was overwhelmed. "America, what a wonderful country," she whispered to me in Yiddish.

United Artists forgave me for going over budget. *The Vikings* was the fifth highest-grossing film of 1958—it earned $7 million domestically and $13 million worldwide, which were huge numbers in those days.

Anne's production, too, was a success. I was home for the birth of our second son, Eric Anthony Douglas, on June 21, 1958, his name a souvenir of the adventure where he was conceived.

Then I left for London. On July 8, 1958, *The Vikings* had a royal gala premiere in Leicester Square, London. HRH Prince Philip represented the Queen, and Princess Margaret joined him in the receiving line. Anne sent me this cable for the occasion:

=DARLING DADDY OUR LONELY LITTLE VIKING FAMILY IS WISHING YOU ALL THE BEST OF LUCK FOR TONIGHT WE LOVE YOU AND MISS YOU VERY MUCH= PETER ERIC AND MOMMIE=

The next day I wrote Anne about my triumphant evening:

Darling—
Last night was the premiere and I'm not over it yet. Everyone seems to agree that it went very well. I am sending you the clippings. I was more nervous than I was at any other premiere— probably because of Prince Philip. He was most charming.

The party was a real smash—by far, the best party of all. The way they had the place decorated was fantastic. I've become a junior Mike Todd.

Now that it's over, I want to settle down and just work on my script.

I loved your letter written on the yellow paper. It made me so homesick. I miss you all so much tonight.

*By the way, Richard Gully [*an aristocratic British expatriate doing society p.r. in Beverly Hills*], Princess Pignatelli and a couple of French dames came to the opening. This morning, Richard dropped off a little gift for you—a couple of Hermès scarves. I thought that was very considerate of him.*

*This is such a well-located place [*27 Eaton Square, Belgravia*]. So many people live near here. The Oliviers live just across the square, the Harmsworths around the corner, etc.*

Rehearsals are going fairly well. But I've got to start doing some work.

With Peter and Baby Eric

> *It's 11—I had dinner home tonight—very good. And so far, that butler-driver is ideal! If he keeps up, you will want to get him. I'm waiting for the catch, because he does every-thing—knows wines, menus, serves perfectly, etc., etc.*
>
> *I love you my love and I miss you very much. I'm tired and I'll try to sleep now with nice dreams of you, Peter, and Eric.*
>
> *—K.*

ANNE:

I was used to our periodic separations. Peter was not. Kirk and I spoke every Sunday by phone, but placing a call overseas was difficult. The operator had to call when the line was clear. Sometimes it took hours. Between that and the eight-hour time difference, Peter was often asleep and couldn't speak with his daddy. But it was wonderful when we connected.

Dear Darling,

Thank God for that Edison invention, or was it Bell—the Telephone! It was so good to talk to you, love. I was so full with beautiful thoughts and feelings.

I looked at my two boys—my beautiful house, my gorgeous car, at all the servants and I say to myself—

Gee—that Douglas, he sure is lucky! No, Sweetheart, I should be so grateful that I don't have the time for anything else. Darling, let us appreciate it together and remind each other constantly when some unpleasant moments occur.

For a change I am in bed waiting for Eric to go to the source! I had two beers, so there should be plenty! Peter told me tonight very seriously: "Mommy—you want to do me a favor? Tell my Daddy to come home!"

I had a little radio on, not very loud. Peter came storming into my room, turned it off and said: "It is going to wake my baby brother up!" Oh, my Darling, how proud I am of our two boys! And how proud I am of myself—and YOU.

I'm looking at Eric right now lying there beside me and eating—you know he is beautiful and, you know, he looks very much like me! I shall study him very carefully and as soon as I discover something which looks like you I will let you know!!

I am delighted that you like your little bachelor flat and also the butler. Don't worry about the Bentley. Darling, if you love the car that much we shall sell Peter's bicycle, his Hot Rod Racer, Eric's buggy, and even your Karmann Ghia!

You seem to have such a busy social schedule. They love you, Sweetheart. Have good rehearsals from tomorrow on. Miss me, baby, miss me! Take good care of everything good in you—clear out everything bad. Watch out for those girls who are after you.

I love you very much! Stolz

KIRK:

Larry Olivier was going through a rough time with his wife, Vivien Leigh. She was bipolar. In 1958, treatments such as lithium were not widespread and the disease is very complex. Years later, Anne and I learned that our sweet baby Eric had the same affliction.

Larry was very gentle with Vivien, but she could be vicious to him in public. In private she also made his life hell—sometimes raging at him through the night. Vivien's hypersexuality—a common symptom—was also a problem. She would proposition male dinner guests even when she and Larry were hosting them. She did it with me. Despite the strains at home, Larry remained the consummate professional. He was the best thing in *The Devil's Disciple*, which should have been a much better film than it turned out to be.

One day Larry approached me at the studio. He was in charge of entertainment for the Motion Picture Relief Fund's annual charity gala, the "Night of a Hundred Stars." Would Burt and I participate in the July 24 event?

Four months before, Burt and I had done a song-and-dance routine, "It's Great Not to be Nominated," at the thirtieth annual Academy Awards which were televised on March 26, 1958. (Almost sixty years later, I was able to watch it on YouTube.)

We thought we could do something similar at the Palladium. We settled on an old English music hall number, and finished with me standing on Burt's shoulders and somersaulting in unison off the stage.

"Boit" and "Koik" made a good team. *The Devil's Disciple* was our third picture of the seven we would eventually make, plus our star turn in the play *The Boys of Autumn*. When I offered Burt a lead role in *Seven Days in May*, I magnanimously said, "You can have whichever part you want. I'll play the other." Naturally, he picked the one I really wanted. It's always more fun to play the bad guy.

I wrote Anne on July 19 about the upcoming show:

Darling—

This is just about an hour after our phone conversation. How nice to talk to you and Peter!

How often I think that if I weren't married to you, I'd be in awful shape. I'd be a bum and a drunkard without you. And the awful thing is I keep needing you more and more as I get older!

Larry is terrific in his part. I feel I still need so much work to do on mine, but maybe it'll begin to come later on.

Burt and I have been rehearsing our number for the Night of 100 Stars. We will be dressed up like typical Englishmen with bowler hats and umbrellas and we sing a song called "Maybe It's Because I'm a Londoner."

I'll tell you all about my trip to Spain when I get back. [I was headed to the San Sebastian Film Festival.]

Ah, I almost forgot to thank you for the new money clip with the new initials. Now we can't have more kids, because there's no room for more initials!

Goodnight, my love—and all my love!— *K.*

ANNE:

I answered at once:

Mon Chéri,

I hope you will find this letter when you get back from your Spanish escapade! God, am I sorry I can't be with you to visit a new country together for the first time! Well, that's motherhood for you—no regrets—just comments.

Eric is 8.6 ounces today—not one month old and gained over 1 pound. I am so proud of myself. You would see a tremendous change in him. His hair is very light blond and his complexion like Peter. Peter is such a wunderkind. When I look at him, I drool. He is so bright and so tender underneath his roughness.

I had a long talk with Eddie Lewis today. Eddie will write to you in detail, but what I can see, as a matter of fact what I always say—I don't see the possibility for you to stay with R & N [Rosenthal & Norton]. It is much too involved to explain it to you in detail, but financially it is a great risk. The fee they have charged you for the last five years is outrageous and the legal advice was more than poor! Conclusions are up to you! This has been checked by authorized people, Lew Wasserman, Bautzer, etc.—My humble little opinion comes only trailing behind! No decision should be taken while you are abroad—therefore everything has to come to a standstill until you return.

I miss you and I adore you.

Peter & Eric & Mommy

Kirk was urging me to come to England as soon as the doctor gave his okay. It was a hard decision for me, but eventually I decided my "big boy" needed me as much as my little ones. The children would be in good hands with nannies and the rest of our household staff. By the end of July I was weaning Eric to a bottle so I could travel. I described the process to Kirk in this excerpt from my letter of July 29:

My Darling,

. . . I feel a little better today but I still have ice packs around me and continue to take those awful pills. I think by tomorrow I will be a lot better. Maybe God is punishing me for trying to dry up the good milk Eric is supposed to get! But in order for me to leave after my six weeks checkup, I had to do it and also when I see him so happy with his bottle and myself so miserable being separated from you—there is no pain which can stop me!!

KIRK:

I had given Howard Fast's *Spartacus* to Sir Laurence after the Palladium triumph where Burt and I were the highlight of the evening. He said he was fascinated by the book. Eddie Lewis was bringing the first-draft screenplay to London the following week. We hoped Larry would like it enough to sign on as director and play Crassus. At this stage, we were using the fiction that Sam Jackson was Eddie Lewis. Neither of us were comfortable with the ruse, especially when Larry complimented Eddie on his masterful writing.

My agent, Lew Wasserman—one of the most powerful men in Hollywood—also represented Olivier as well as Charles Laughton and Peter Ustinov. I already knew United Artists would not finance *Spartacus*. They had announced a new Roman spectacle called *The Gladiators* with Marty Ritt as director and starring Yul Brynner. Lew told me they, too, were going after my dream cast so it was imperative I get my script to them first. Lew said not to worry. He would get Universal to back my project and he would "sell" his clients on being in the picture. No one yet knew that Lew was in the process of buying the studio. Lew cautioned me not to let anyone know my screenwriter was Dalton Trumbo, the blacklisted scribe who had spent a year in prison for defying the HUAC almost a decade before.

ANNE:

Kirk had promised me after the Mike Todd tragedy that he would always trust my instincts. This didn't apply to Sam Norton. He was moving a few responsibilities away from him, although Sam was still taking 10 percent of Kirk's gross earnings, and his law firm, Rosenthal and Norton, was extracting 10 percent more. I didn't trust them, or their partner, Fitzgerald, who was the investment banker.

I asked Greg Bautzer: "Can raising questions about Sam backfire on me because I don't have the complete proof?" Greg advised me to discuss it with one of Kirk's confidantes and ask, "What should we do to have the books checked?"

That's when I went to Eddie Lewis and said: "I don't trust Sam Norton, but what am I going to do about it?"

"Let's call Price Waterhouse and have the books examined and you stay out of it," Eddie recommended. I got the report just before I left for England, but I didn't want to upset Kirk until he got home and we could work out a strategy with a new lawyer.

KIRK:

I'm glad I didn't know. I was getting rosy letters from Sam all the time about my wonderful investments: "Oil continues to flow like liquor at a fireman's ball," he wrote in one.

The Devil's Disciple was plodding along, a new director at the helm. Anne's visit seemed near but not near enough when I dashed off this letter to her on August 5, 1958:

> *Darling—*
>
> *It was good to talk to you last night. I am writing this at the studio between shots. This is the first day with the new director—Guy Hamilton. I think he'll be fine.*
>
> *They just called me for a shot. I'll be back—We just broke for lunch and I'm waiting here in my dressing room for it.*
>
> *I can't believe Eric is now ten pounds. He must look quite different. Why don't you take a photo and send it to me.*
>
> *The first weekend you arrive, I will try to line up some place in the country—that will give you a chance to rest a bit because the change in hours will knock you out. Then we can go to the Brussels Fair for one weekend and Paris for the other. When we go to Paris, you can leave a few days earlier and I will meet you there Friday night.*
>
> *I miss you and the kids so much that sometimes I ache.*
>
> *When Eric gets a little older, I would like to arrange that we always travel together except for short periods of time. Just think, darling, this is our family. We're very lucky.*
>
> *Tomorrow we're going to shoot outdoors. I hope the weather is good.*
>
> *I played one set of singles this weekend—didn't do too*

well. I'm at that age, honey. I've got to work to keep my weight and stay in condition.

Am I glad I have none of the production problems on this picture. In fact, from now on I want to have very little to do with any production problem even if the picture is in my company.

I'm anxious to read the script of "Spartacus" if it's that good. I'll be anxious to know what you think of it.

Get all the sunshine you can, because there isn't too much here. With your clothes, remember that we'll be going into fall weather.

By the way, did I tell you that I won one of the prizes for best acting in The Vikings *at the San Sebastian festival? I felt embarrassed about it.*

You sounded in good spirits when I talked to you on the phone. Stay that way! I love you very, very, very, very much my darling.

—K

ANNE:

Our letters crossed. I, too, was writing to Kirk on August 5. I had just finished reading the first draft of Dalton's—I mean Sam Jackson's—screenplay:

My Darling,

In the script of Spartacus *it says on page 61—I love you—I give myself to you—Forbid me ever to leave you!! The only hope I have is that your answer, Kirk, will be "I forbid you!!"*

I just came home from dinner at Perino's with Sammy and Gloria Cahn. Afterwards to the Cocoanut Grove—closing night of Judy Garland. It was a great thrill. I loved her and she is a fantastic performer. Drinks after the show in her bungalow. Liz Taylor—15 pounds heavier—with Arthur

Loew Jr. (serious romance). Betty Bacall, Doris [Day] and Marty Melcher, etc.

You won't believe it but I read Spartacus, *all 223 pages. It was very interesting to read but I don't know enough about this kind of script or picture to judge if it is fantastic or formidable! Lew Wasserman thinks it is great and Eddie and Stan think the same way.*

I cancelled my reservation for the 18th today with a tear in my eye and start to count the days up to the 21st. How I will manage to leave Peter and Eric I don't know yet, but I know I will—because my big son needs me more now, I know—and I need him badly. All evening, when I was enjoying myself so much, I was feeling sad because it would have been so much better with you!

I finished my checkup. I can play tennis again, take massages, do exercises and f—! The latter will have to wait.

Tomorrow I take Peter to the beach. We will have lunch there and come home before the traffic.

I am installing a burglar alarm in the house—directly relayed to the police in Beverly Hills. Three buttons. One in the nurse's room, maid's room, and our room. I feel better this way and I think it is wise anyway.

Mon Chéri, keep up the wonderful thoughts you have about me. I am really a dreamboat and you are a lovely man—because I am in love with you.

Stolz

KIRK:

Things were moving along nicely on *Spartacus*. Larry agreed to direct. Only one snafu: he wanted to play Spartacus. He had a completely different vision of the role than I did, but I'd leave it up to Lew to sort it out. On August 12, I wrote to Anne again:

Darling—

Your letter this morning with the 3 pictures was a delight. I can't get over how big Peter looks. He's really going to be a strapping boy. And Eric, he's changed so! He's so much bigger.

Peter Ustinov just called from Switzerland. He's excited about the script and wants to play the part. We are now waiting to hear from Laughton.

By the way, Eddie told me about your $10 bet. You lose, honey. Perhaps it's taken me a long time to see it, but my relationship with Sam is impossible. In fact, I don't see how he can represent me even as a lawyer! I've got to have peace of mind in this area for both of us.

I'm writing this on the set waiting for my next shot. The picture is going along well but I can't work up much excitement for it! I have much more for Spartacus.

The Oliviers invited us out to the country, but I didn't want to make a definite date until you arrive. Do you realize how important you are to me? If you did, you would take better care of yourself for my sake. I need you very much—and everything I do is for you and our family.

If Spartacus *ever comes off the way I hope—this will be the picture with which we can make our world tour.*

It is thundering outside—I wish you were here so that you could be frightened and I would cuddle you.

Stop complaining about lack of letters. The boss is thinking so hard about you that often I can't write.

I love you and the boys madly!—K

P.S. Like Eric, I have gas and constipation. I need to be breast-fed!

Just over a week later, Anne was finally on her way to London. While she was en route I wrote her an impassioned love letter in anticipation of our reunion. As of the time of this writing, we have been married more than sixty-two years and my unabated admiration and need for this remarkable woman still astounds me. I shake my head at the line I wrote on August 21, 1958: "if we live to be a hundred, there will still be so many unsaid things." As I have now reached that milestone, I can attest that it's still true.

My darling wife—

As I write this, you are thousands of feet above the earth— sleeping peacefully I hope—but racing toward me. I say "racing" because they say airplanes fly so fast. To me, it seems you are creeping.

Why am I writing? You will be here soon. But I know that when you get here, we will still not have time to say all the things we want to say to each other. In fact, if we live to be a hundred, there will still be so many unsaid things which is just as well, perhaps, because then, if there is a life after death, we will have many things to talk about later.

As I write, I realize that I have been the happiest in my life with you—talking with you or just being with you. Really, I should talk more with you because je me suis rendu compte_ *[I figured out] that you fell in love with me on an evening in Paris in my apartment_near the Bois while I talked. It was about five or six or seven—I don't remember. All I know is that I did most of the talking, you listened, and I felt that parts of you that had been closed for so long opened up, until it seemed that all of your pores were open too—and every part of you was ready to receive me. I don't know what makes me think of that evening. Do you remember?*

Perhaps it's strange that I should write about <u>when</u> *I think* <u>you</u> *fell in love with* <u>me</u>*! It's just that it's important for me always to know and feel that you love me. Sometimes, you close up parts of yourself and then I'm not sure whether or not you take your love for me behind that barrier that can spring up so suddenly.*

It's also important to _me_ that you know and feel that I love you _always_. Sometimes I sense that you are not sure. You must be sure always—because your love for me would be less if you didn't know how much I love you in return.

When did I fall in love with you? I don't know. Unfortunately, with me, I become aware of love only through a sense of loss. I remember how anxious I was for you to join me in Rome. I remember too well when you were in the south of France and I was in Paris with Pier Angeli. Suddenly my love for you came over me like a tidal wave and I called you. I remember when I came back to America and you stayed in Europe—How I missed you then and how I miss you now! I want to change that—I want to be more aware of my love for you when you are with me than to realize how deep my love for you by my sense of loss when we are apart.

But you must realize—this right hand of mine that writes these words, I take for granted. But oh how I would miss it if it were cut off!

How silly I am! You will be here tomorrow and I am writing you a longer letter than when we are apart! Maybe I should save this letter for some later time, when you rebuke me for my short letters. But, no, I want you to have this now because I hope we will be seldom separated in the future. But more important, I want you to know _now_, when I am _near_ you, not thousands of miles away, that I love you, my darling wife, with all my heart!

—K.

CHAPTER EIGHT

Becoming Spartacus

KIRK:

I came back from England in fine spirits. That lasted for about thirty-six hours. As soon as Anne felt I was rested, she sat me down and showed me how right she had been in her fears about Sam. He had played me for an absolute fool—another father who had taken my hard-earned money the way Harry took Issur's. This was worse, because Pa never suggested he had my best interests at heart; Sam always insisted I came first.

I had put my family's future in jeopardy by not listening to Anne. In brief, this is what the Price Waterhouse audit uncovered: I had no money in the bank. I owed the IRS $750,000. The eighteen months I had spent overseas did not qualify for the tax-free income break. My "solid investments" were all funneled through dummy corporations owned by Sam Norton. Sam had even cross-collateralized the profits from *The Indian Fighter* with the losses from *Spring Reunion*, leaving a zero balance.

I had made some twenty-seven pictures with Sam in charge of my income. He became a wealthy man. I was broke and in debt. In my righteous wrath, I wanted to confront him with my fists rather than my brains.

I certainly had right on my side. Even better, thank God, I had Anne there. We went to the new lawyer she had retained. He gave us wonderful advice, but it would be up to me—the trained actor—to implement the plan.

A few days later I stormed into Sam's office, waving the Price Water-house report in front of him. I threatened to send him to jail. Sam pan-icked. "I'll kill myself," he cried, matching my theatrics. I put down the stick and waved the carrot: "Sam, I know that greedy *gonif* Jerry was behind this. I don't want him to make any more money off of me. If you sign a paper saying that Rosenthal & Norton relinquish all rights to commissions, percentages or fees on *The Vikings* and any of my future income, you and I will start fresh. You can be president of Bryna, han-dling all my business and producing my films. That's how we'll both get back at Jerry."

Within the hour, I walked out of Rosenthal & Norton, free from any further rape of my income. I never spoke to Sam again. We could only make Sam liable for $200,000 of what he'd stolen. It was a fraction of our loss, but it was the only money we could prove he had used to buy things for himself and his family. The rest of his assets—which I had paid for—he put in his wife's name.

ANNE:

We used the profits from *The Vikings* to pay off the IRS. Our for-tunes now depended on *Spartacus*. It was budgeted at $4 million. The final cost was $12 million—about $750,000 more than Lew Wasserman's MCA had paid for the whole of Universal's 367 acres. If *Spartacus* had bombed, Lew might have turned the studio into tract housing the way, decades later, Century City resulted from Marvin Davis's sale of Twenti-eth Century-Fox's huge back lot.

Kirk was still trying to cast *Spartacus*. He was thrilled that Ustinov and even Charles Laughton—who was disdainful of the script when he first saw it in London—had signed their contracts. Lew had been right when he said Laughton needed the money. There was still no final com-mitment from Olivier, however. Kirk had mixed feelings about Sir Lau-rence. He wanted him to direct, but certainly didn't want him to take the title role. Finally, the letter from London arrived at the office. Kirk came home that day, all smiles, waving Larry's letter in front of me. He read me the salient information:

. . . I have now contracted myself to go to Stratford-on-Avon for the fourth play of the season next year, which is Coriolanus *and to start rehearsing in June. I imagine this decision will fairly knock me out for any further consideration as director of the film. If, however, you can still see your way to improving the part of Crassus in relation to the other three roles, then I should be more than happy to look at it again as it is such a gallant enterprise and one I should be extremely proud to be part of. Could you be so kind as to let me see something just as soon as you possibly can?*

KIRK:

Now all I had to worry about was getting a director acceptable to both the studio and me; casting Spartacus's love, Varinia; and getting a finished script. We would start filming in late January 1959—a new year.

I certainly wasn't sorry to turn the page on the old one. I had escaped Mike Todd's fate in March only to be brought low six months later by the betrayal of Sam Norton and my precarious financial position. But the gods weren't through punishing me yet. My beloved Ma, the namesake of the Bryna Company, died in mid-December. Her last wish was not to be buried with Pa.

I had no time to feel sorry for myself. I had too much on my plate. By mid-January my British actors and I were at Universal for costume fittings and to meet the director approved by Universal and Lew Wasserman, Anthony Mann. I didn't think he was right for the project, but I didn't have any better suggestions. We had more than a hundred people on payroll, and already the budget had risen to $5 million. We needed to forge ahead. For the role of Varinia, I went with Sabine Bethmann, a young actress unknown outside of Germany. Her English was on a par with Elsa Martinelli's when I put her in *The Indian Fighter*.

We shot the first scenes in Death Valley. Within three weeks, it became apparent that Anthony Mann had lost control of the production. All of my English superstars had directed films, and they all had their own ideas. Within that short framework of time, the budget had risen still another million dollars. Universal's production chief Eddie Muhl told me to fire Tony Mann. I felt bad as Tony was a good man, but he had never been right for this picture. I think he was actually relieved when I let him go on Friday the 13th of February.

Bad luck for the budget if I couldn't find a new director quickly. Luckily, Stanley Kubrick found himself unexpectedly at liberty. He was in L.A. to direct Marlon Brando's *One-Eyed Jacks*, but after waffling for a few months, Brando decided to direct the film himself. I tracked down Stanley, who was playing poker at Marty Ritt's house. Marty, too, was unemployed after United Artists pulled the plug on *The Gladiators*. I made Stanley an offer he couldn't refuse: $150,000—the biggest payday of his career and the biggest budget of any film he had ever directed. I messengered the script to his hotel and told him to be at Universal on Monday.

I should have had cameras rolling to capture the cast's expressions when I introduced the boy from the Bronx—ill-dressed and ill at ease, not looking anywhere near his thirty years. But Stanley and his supreme ego would be more than a match for all of them. We went back to work.

That is, all of us but Sabine Bethmann. Stanley said she couldn't act and proved it to me in a rather cruel fashion. Again, I was faced with one of my least favorite parts of being the boss: letting someone go. I called Jean Simmons, who lived with her husband, Stewart Granger, on a ranch in Arizona, and asked if she was still interested in the role. (I had rejected her earlier because of my stubborn belief that the Romans should be English, the slaves anything but.)

After this rocky and costly beginning, I breathed a sigh of relief. We used Anthony Mann's footage, even though Stanley wanted to shoot everything again. Then real life intruded on our tight schedule: Jean had an operation that kept her away for six weeks; Tony Curtis snapped his Achilles heel playing tennis with me in Palm Springs; and I finally collapsed from exhaustion and was ordered to rest for ten days.

I called these setbacks the "Curse of Spartacus." The budget was now at $7 million and rising. It didn't help that Stanley was proving even more difficult than he had been on *Paths of Glory*. I had to keep him in line without dampening his creative genius or letting my annoyance with him disrupt the picture.

In the midst of all this, media speculation escalated about who was really writing *Spartacus*. Walter Winchell and the *Hollywood Reporter* printed that Dalton Trumbo was Sam Jackson. It was becoming the worst-kept secret in Hollywood. I had to deny the rumors to Universal's production head, Eddie Muhl, while secretly promising Dalton I would tell the studio when it was too late for them to pull the plug. When it came time to discuss screenplay credit, Stanley volunteered that he would "help us out by letting us use his name." I was appalled that he would want to take credit for another man's work. I swore to "Sam" he would see the words Dalton Trumbo on the screen in large letters when the picture opened.

ANNE:

Although Eddie Lewis was doing his best to relieve Kirk of day-to-day problems, when it came down to the crunch, the buck stopped with Kirk. He was constantly putting out fires as well as performing the most dangerous stunts of his career. My job was to calm him down, to listen, and reassure. But his worry was contagious. After all, I knew too well how precarious our financial position was and how much depended on the success of *Spartacus*.

Kirk would vent to me at night about the problems and the ego clashes. Charles Laughton threatened to sue Kirk personally because he thought his part had been reduced. Stanley's arrogance was intolerable. Kirk worried if he would still have a career if he admitted that Dalton Trumbo was his screenwriter. Did Hedda Hopper really have the power to destroy him? Neither of us was sleeping well.

KIRK:

Stanley continued to squander money on retakes and experimental shots. We had now spent over $8 million and Stanley didn't care. It became easier to communicate with him by memo. In my files at the University of Wisconsin are myriad examples of this sometimes contentious correspondence. Here's one I sent him with the outline of a scene I thought would have a great dramatic impact when the Roman army conquered the Spartacus troops:

> *. . . The battle is over and in a gully near the battlefield, all the prisoners are being rounded up; a large group of them are already chained and are sitting around, waiting for the next move . . .*
>
> *At a distance, on a rise, sits the noble Crassus on his white horse. He is surveying the assembly of prisoners . . . next to him is one of his generals. At a signal from Crassus, his subordinate general rides down with a group of slaves.*
>
> *In a loud voice, he announces to them that whoever identifies the living or dead body of Spartacus will be set free.*
>
> *There is a sudden, silent hush over all the prisoners. Spartacus gets up . . .*
>
> *Suddenly, Antoninus jumps up with his arm waving, "I am Spartacus!" In short order, the hundreds and hundreds of slaves are all jumping up, yelling in a happy vein, "I am Spartacus!"*
>
> *Crassus stands alone, surveying this mockery of his victory by a group of doomed men. He whirls away on his horse, in his ears the crescendo of exultant slaves all yelling in unison . . . "Spartacus . . . Spartacus . . . Spartacus!"*

I waited to hear what Stanley thought, but he didn't bother to reply. I seethed. I confronted him. First, I castigated him on his lack of respect for the crew and cast. In those days, directors dressed formally when they were working. Stanley had worn an ill-fitting and none-too-pristine blazer with baggy khaki pants every day since he came on board.

"It would help if you changed your clothes now and then," I said, staring down at him from atop a huge stallion. "The crew doesn't think you respect them."

Left to right: Woody Strode, Stanley Kubrick, and Kirk prior to the Spartacus gladiator fight

"I don't," he replied.

Now I really blew up. "You're going to wear new clothes tomorrow. Understand me?" By this time, my horse had backed him up against a wall.

I continued. "There's something else I want you to understand. When I send you a memo about shooting a scene, I at least expect an answer. You haven't bothered to respond about the 'I am Spartacus' scene I suggested."

Stanley had no charm. He said bluntly, "I don't want to do it. It's a stupid idea."

I exploded. Using a lot of expletives, I said, "This *may* be a stupid idea but we're going to shoot it. If it doesn't work, we'll cut it out."

I hated acting like a bully, but Stanley needed to learn how things were done when so much money was on the line. Sometimes he forgot that making a film was a collaborative effort and that all of us were experienced professionals.

We had budgeted for five months—but that was before Stanley insisted we create battle scenes to be shot in Spain using Generalissimo Franco's armies. Universal approved the additional money—bringing the cost up to $11 million—and Stanley spent the month of November 1959 in Iberia. I stayed in California.

ANNE:

Kirk was enjoying that break from Stanley. It was amazing how much tension this talented young man added to our lives. At one point, Kirk was so irritated with him that I suggested they both air their grievances to a neutral party. Kirk made an appointment for them with Dr. Herbert Kupper, our starstruck psychiatrist.

Kirk wasn't sure it helped the situation, but Dr. Kupper gave Stanley a gift. He recommended a German novella by Arthur Schnitzler to him, saying it would make a good movie. It took forty years, but that 1926 story became the basis for *Eyes Wide Shut*, Stanley's last film. It was a flop.

KIRK:

I lived with *Spartacus* for some three years, and it is still the film most associated with me. I was crucified in the movie and I was crucified by the far right extremists, like Hedda Hopper, who believed the blacklist should go on forever. Despite Universal's forty-four unauthorized cuts to the print that was released, it still was a financial and critical success, thanks to Stanley's extraordinary talent as a filmmaker. Neither of us wanted to work together ever again, but despite all, I credit him with launching *Spartacus* into film immortality.

Spartacus opened at the DeMille Theater in New York on October 6, 1960. It premiered at the Pantages Theater in Hollywood two weeks later. Anne organized the event as a benefit for the Women's Guild of Cedars of Lebanon Hospital, a group she had been involved with since she became my wife. The studios were used to free tickets. Anne changed all that. She insisted they pay $100 for each seat, as well as make a contribution to the Guild. She raised more than $100,000 for the hospital's free bed program. I was, as always, very proud of her.

CLOCKWISE FROM TOP LEFT: *Anne, age fourteen, at boarding school in Switzerland. • Anne's beloved childhood governess, Trulla. • A summer snap of Anne's sister Inge with their mother. • Beauty on the beach—relaxing between crises at Cannes.*

CLOCKWISE FROM TOP LEFT: *Champion wrestler Izzy Demsky (top row, second from left) with his teammates at St. Lawrence University. • Young actor ready to work—Kirk's 1941 American Academy of Dramatic Arts graduation photo. • Oh, brother! Kirk and his six sisters.*

CLOCKWISE FROM TOP LEFT: *Kirk and Frances Woodward in a soon-to-be-forgotten play on Broadway. • A star is born: A 1946 publicity still of producer Hal Wallis with the Broadway actor he signed for* The Strange Love of Martha Ivers. *• Anatole (Tola) Litvak, director of* Act of Love *(1953) and Anne's good friend, during Klosters, Switzerland holiday (1954). • Anne and Anthony Quinn in Rome, 1953, during the filming of* Ulysses.

CLOCKWISE FROM TOP LEFT: *Anne and her "awful wedded husband" after exchanging vows in Las Vegas.* • *Daddy shows Peter the view from the top.* • *Eric and Peter at home in Beverly Hills with their parents and maternal grandmother.*

FROM TOP: *All-star entertainment at SHARE Boomtown gala: (left to right) Tony Martin, Dean Martin, Kirk, Jimmy Durante, and Tony Curtis. • Laurence Olivier chats backstage at the Palladium with "Boit" and "Koik" before they do their act at the "Night of 100 Stars," July 24, 1958. • Cyd Charisse, Kirk, columnist Louella Parsons, and party hosts Denise and Vincente Minnelli at a celebration for the cast of Two Weeks in Another Town (1962).*

CLOCKWISE FROM TOP LEFT: *Commanding both sides of Broadway in 1963 with a revival of 20,000 Leagues Under the Sea playing across from One Flew Over the Cuckoo's Nest. • Airport reception and press conference at Haneda Airport, Japan. • Inaugurating the Lutheran World Federation's Mobile Canteen for Child Feeding in Hong Kong, March 12, 1964.*

CLOCKWISE FROM TOP LEFT: *Meeting Indira Ghandi on a goodwill stop in India, March 26, 1964. • Anne and Kirk portrait by Arthur Zinn, 1964 • Anne gets a lesson in traditional dance techniques at the Royal Dancing School in Thailand, March 6, 1964.*

CLOCKWISE FROM TOP LEFT: *Arriving in Poland on an eastern European goodwill tour, April 1, 1966. • In Harm's Way (1965) stars John (never Duke) Wayne and Kirk in Hawaii, waiting for the cameras to roll. • Casting a giant shadow in Israel, Kirk and Yul Brynner between takes with little Eric and Anne, 1966.*

FROM TOP: Apollo 14 *astronauts Edgar Mitchell and Alan Shepherd have a down-to-earth moment with Anne and Kirk at the Kennedy Space Center the day before the launch on January 31, 1971. • Henry Fonda and Kirk on location in Australia for filming of* There Was a Crooked Man (1970). *• Kirk and Danny Kaye say "mazel tov" to Jimmy Cagney, AFI Life Achievement Award winner in 1974.*

FROM TOP:
Thomas Dye School moms Nancy Reagan and Anne Douglas work the hot dog booth at the annual fair. • Greeting President Reagan at Sunnylands New Year's Eve, 1976: (left to right) Ambassador Walter Annenberg, Anne, and Kirk. • Kirk and Helen Hayes with Lady Bird Johnson at the Johnson Library on December 11, 1977, to celebrate her sixty-fifth birthday with a reading of the Johnsons' love letters.

FROM TOP: *Kirk takes a break from filming* The Chosen *in Jerusalem in 1977 to offer a prayer at the Wailing Wall.* • *Coffee at the White House with First Lady Nancy Reagan.*

To Kirk –
Drop by any time for coffee!
Best – Nancy

In the image, handwritten inscription reads:

To my Friend Kirk,
Best wishes
28/12/1988

CLOCKWISE FROM TOP LEFT: *Anne's sister Merle and Kirk on Christmas Day, 1987, in Palm Springs. • Kirk with Hollywood's bipartisan newlyweds, Kennedy offspring Maria Shriver and Arnold Schwarzenegger. • Egyptian President Anwar Sadat became a good friend of the Douglases after their visit in 1988.*

CLOCKWISE FROM TOP LEFT: *Anne and Kirk, photographed by friend Roddy McDowall.* • *Kennedy Center Honorees of 1994. Top: Kirk Douglas, Aretha Franklin, Pete Seeger, and seated: Harold Prince and Morton Gould.* • *At home after the 1996 Oscars, the family celebrates Kirk's post-stroke appearance.*

CLOCKWISE FROM TOP LEFT: *Celebrating Tel Aviv's fiftieth anniversary with Sally Field and Goldie Hawn.* • *Anne visits Kirk on the set of Diamonds (1999), his first film post-stroke.* • *Michael and Catherine Zeta-Jones hear some words of wisdom from the Bar Mitzvah "boy."*

The plaque reads:

פארק דאגלס
לזכר יצחק רבין
הוקם באמצעות קרן תל אביב לפיתוח

DOUGLAS PARK
IN MEMORY OF
YITZHAK RABIN
ESTABLISHED BY THE
TEL AVIV FOUNDATION
1997

CLOCKWISE FROM TOP LEFT: *Kirk and Don Rickles share Jewish jokes at Kirk's second Bar Mitzvah, at age eighty-three. • "Douglas of Arabia" rides while Anne walks through Petra with the Jordanian Minister of Culture during a 2000 visit with King Abdullah and Queen Rania. • Kirk visits Douglas Park in 2000.*

CLOCKWISE FROM TOP: *With "mishpucha" (family) at Kirk and Anne's fiftieth anniversary and second wedding.* • *A big grin from the new centenarian at his birthday bash, December 9, 2016.* • *A tender moment between Anne and Lauren Bacall during the Douglases' Jewish wedding on May 29, 2004.*

Spartacus *premiere party, Rome, with Eddie Fisher and Elizabeth Taylor*

Hedda Hopper became a paper tiger. Her campaign to boycott my film fizzled. A few American Legion diehards made a half-hearted attempt to picket. The public ignored them. Then the popular new president of the United States, John Fitzgerald Kennedy, slipped into the Warner Theater in Washington on Wednesday, February 3, 1961, a few weeks after moving into the White House. He hoped no one would notice his arrival with his old navy buddy Paul B. (Red) Fay, the new undersecretary of the navy. But his days of going anywhere unnoticed were gone forever. When asked how he liked *Spartacus*, he declared it a fine film. The box office continued to boom.

ANNE:

Kirk kept his word to me. We went to many countries to promote the film. In Rome, Elizabeth Taylor hosted the *Spartacus* premiere party for us. She was making *Cleopatra* and was the biggest publicity magnet in the world because of her torrid love affair with Richard Burton. Her poor husband Eddie Fisher was trying to make the best of what was, undoubtedly, an uncomfortable evening for him.

I hoped our lives would calm down a bit before Kirk left in May to make *The Last Sunset* in Mexico. Dalton Trumbo, now able to use his name again, had written the script, although he still called himself Sam when he phoned us. He went down to Mexico with Kirk, now that he had delivered the script of *Exodus* to Otto Preminger.

Always the publicity hound, Otto fired his original blacklisted writer Albert Maltz and hired Dalton as soon as his brother, Ingo, who was Trumbo's agent, told him Kirk was going to put Dalton's given name on *Spartacus*. Otto couldn't resist the opportunity to grab credit by announcing Dalton Trumbo was writing *Exodus*. He loved telling people he broke the blacklist and Kirk was only following his lead.

Kirk felt the script for *The Last Sunset* would have been better if Dalton hadn't been writing Otto's script at the same time. He had become very fond of "Sam," who was also turning the book of *The Last Cowboy* into a screenplay for what would become Kirk's favorite of all his films, *Lonely Are the Brave*.

I was still dealing with the fallout from the other Sam we had banished from our lives. For a while, Sam Norton paid us $2,500 a month, trying all the while to worm his way back into our good graces. He dogged me at the SHARE Boomtown party, an annual charity event still going strong after all these years. I mentioned it in my letter to Kirk:

> *Friday the 13th*
>
> *God, you lucky, lucky man! Here it is 2:30 a.m. I just got home from the Share party. I sat at the table between Cantinflas and Yves Montand. I looked at Frank, Dean, Sammy*

Davis, Duke Wayne, Tony [Curtis] and Vic Damone on the stage—and who do you think I was thinking of?—you, you silly idiot!

The whole evening, no matter where I looked or went there was Sam Norton! As we were all waiting at the valet stand, he came towards me just as my car arrived. Sam opened the door for me and closed it after I was inside. I said to myself: "This is the most expensive car boy I have ever had!"

The show was great and at the beginning they gave 12 beautiful diplomas to Life Members and you were one of them. I had to go onstage to pick it up—I nearly died!!

Cantinflas was most charming and insists you call him as soon as you get to Mexico City. He would like to give a party for us when I join you.

Merle [Oberon] insists that we should stay at her house in Mexico City. She says she left her chef there and at least six servants. But then she says quite a lot of things.

Peter's teacher called me to school. Apparently since the last two weeks he was fighting with the children again, pounding them in the face. We talked it out and he made big promises. When I drove him and Kelly [Tony Curtis and Janet Leigh's daughter] home from school, he said to her, "Kelly, look at me" and pow—a right pound in her mouth!! I told him he could not watch T.V. So far so good.

As for Eric, he comes out of his room and says, "Daddy, my Daddy." Then I say Daddy bye bye. Then he seems satisfied. But not me!! I miss you so! During the day not so much but after 5:30 p.m. then it starts and by 2:30 a.m. it's unbearable!

—I love you. Stolz.

CHAPTER NINE

Our Hollywood Life

ANNE:

I was in love with America years before I fell in love with Kirk. Through some kindly turn of fate, I was living the American dream with the man of my dreams. How lucky I was.

This really was the New World. In 1954, the United States was only 178 years old; Beverly Hills a mere forty. After living through war and fending for myself in the ancient cities of Europe, I was happy to move to a place where people could shed their old identities and embrace new possibilities. I was enchanted with the warm welcome I received from Kirk's friends. The women were particularly helpful in making me feel at home.

The elegant Fran Stark was my first guardian angel. We had bonded during the visits she and Ray made to Italy and France. Fran was the daughter of Fanny Brice, the beloved comedienne of the *Ziegfeld Follies*. She and her brother Bill, an artist, were raised in Beverly Hills, where Fanny appeared in films and starred as Baby Snooks in America's favorite radio sitcom until her death in 1951.

My official welcome was a large party Kirk organized at the San Ysidro house Fran had decorated so beautifully in tones of black and white. She had purposely left the walls bare, assuming Kirk would want the pleasure of choosing his own artwork. However, with guests coming to appraise both me and the surroundings, I wanted those empty spaces to be warmed with color.

"Take me to a good gallery, Fran. I'll tell the dealer Kirk Douglas is interested in buying a few paintings, but he wants to try them in the house before deciding. You and I can return them after the party."

I borrowed a Chagall canvas of a man on a horse with a rooster and a Vlaminck painting of flowers. Kirk fell in love with both, so the only thing that went back to the gallery was a check. A few years later, after Kirk played the life of Vincent van Gogh in *Lust for Life* and was such a hit, we met Marc Chagall and his wife in the south of France. The Chagalls asked Kirk if he would like to play Marc in a movie, but my husband swore he would never try to inhabit the soul of another painter. We became friends, however, and we acquired a few additional Chagalls directly from them.

Fran was beyond generous. She included me in the luncheons she hosted, and I became her "plus one" whenever friends invited her. She was a prodigious shopper and seemed to have limitless resources. One day Fran asked if Kirk had given me a clothing allowance. It had never occurred to me to ask for one. "Discuss it with him at once," Fran urged. "It will make your life much easier."

I approached my husband carefully: "I don't like to ask you for money each time I shop. Would you be willing to give me a set amount for clothes and necessities?"

Later at the Stark house, Kirk took Fran aside. "Anne wants an allowance. How much do you spend a year?"

She thought for a minute. "About $10,000." I knew she was low-balling it; just that afternoon in a Beverly Hills shop called Hanson's, I watched Fran order $4,500 worth of original designs.

Kirk shook his head. "You spend a lot. I'll give Anne $5,000."

KIRK:

Worth every penny, too. My wife was on the International Best-Dressed List for three years before being elevated permanently to the Fashion Hall of Fame. She was clever with her allowance, just as she was with all our financial dealings. Frankly, Anne was the only good investment I ever made!

Our lifelong friendship with the Starks gave us a lifetime of memories. I'll let Anne tell you about the night we first saw Barbra Streisand perform.

ANNE:

She was about eighteen and singing in one of the small lounges at the Ambassador Hotel in Los Angeles. Barbra was what we call in French *jolie laide*—an unconventional beauty. Her clothes were eccentric but her voice, of course, was magic. This young performer with the strong Brooklyn accent radiated confidence and charisma. Afterward, Barbra and her mother, Diana Kind, joined us. Mama proudly told us she designed and made her daughter's wardrobe.

Fran and I couldn't resist. We dubbed her "Mamabocher"—a play on Mainbocher, the most famous couturier in New York. Of course, we waited until we were on the way home to critique Mamabocher's unique designs.

The next time we saw them was at the restaurant "21" in Manhattan. Barbra had become the toast of Broadway in her debut show, *I Can Get It for You Wholesale* and Ray had just signed her to play his mother-in-law, Fanny Brice, in the musical he was developing. Both Barbra and *Funny Girl*—first on stage and then on film—were enormous hits. I think Mainbocher would have been happy to dress the celebrated young star, but Barbra was wise to stick with her own unique style—thrift store mixed with Hollywood, and perhaps a touch of Mamabocher.

KIRK:

I was interested to see Beverly Hills through Anne's fresh eyes. I had acclimated easily to life in this gilded ghetto where so many of us had punched our ticket to wealth and fame in what was called "the industry." After growing up poor in Yiddish-speaking immigrant families, we had developed a veneer of sophistication with our success. Often, however, we still dropped Yiddish phrases into our conversations because the language is wonderfully pungent.

My pal Walter Matthau, the son of a Russian Jewish peddler, was more comfortable betting on horses than riding them. I cast him as the villain in my first Bryna production, *The Indian Fighter*. Before every take, Walter would curse at his poor horse in Yiddish. Even Jimmy Cagney, one of my idols, greeted me in Yiddish the first time we met at an industry event. I was startled and confused until he explained that, no, he really was Irish, but he learned Yiddish as a child in a mostly Jewish neighborhood. Included in our circle of relocated *landsmen* (compatriots) were the lucky Jews who escaped the Holocaust—among them, my friends Billy Wilder, Peter Lorre, and Ladislaus Bush-Fekete, the Hungarian émigré who wrote with Sidney Sheldon another of my Broadway flops of 1946; I remained friends with both Bush-Fekete and Sheldon.

Sometimes it was easy in Hollywood to forget that anti-Semitism, polite or overt, was still mainstream. Jews ran the major studios. With Anglicized names and beautiful blonde *shiksas* replacing their starter wives, they lived like the wealthy WASPS of their movies: entertaining lavishly at their grand estates; presiding over screenings in projection rooms hung with museum-quality art; voting Republican. I was on their guest lists, but I never felt at my best in these pretentious surroundings. When I married Anne, who was raised in a home like these, she elevated my standing with the leading hostesses. Sam Goldwyn's wife, Frances, and Jack Warner's wife, Ann, were two who told me how much more likeable I was after she came into my life.

ANNE:

I had grown so used to the universal worship of the movie crowd and their lifestyle that it never dawned on me they would not be accepted by the Old Guard of Los Angeles. Their prestige membership clubs—the Jonathan and the California Club downtown, and the Wilshire and

Los Angeles Country Clubs—would not admit Jews or actors. In 1920, the Jews inaugurated Hillcrest Country Club in Beverly Hills, a few blocks from Twentieth Century-Fox studios. By the 1950s, drilling for the rich oil deposits on the property was allowed, and members collected tax-sheltered dividends on their initiation fees. Memberships became so valuable they were willed to heirs. I learned all this and more from my mentor, Anita May, the acknowledged *grande dame* of Beverly Hills society. There are third and fourth generation Mays at Hillcrest to this day.

Anita Keiler May was raised in Kentucky and inherited a fortune built on bourbon. Her husband Tom's family owned a chain of department stores in Saint Louis. The young couple came west in 1922, when Anita asked her father-in-law to let them open the first California branch of the May Company Department Stores in Los Angeles. They moved to the west side of the city, where the movie people and well-to-do Jews were establishing themselves.

It took Dorothy (Buff) Chandler, whose husband Norman was publisher of the *Los Angeles Times*, to bring Jews from Beverly Hills and Brentwood together with gentiles from Pasadena, San Marino, and Hancock Park in a common goal: to raise the enormous sums needed to build the performing arts complex called the Music Center. Buff came from the old Pasadena family that founded Buffum's department store, another successful retail chain.

Mrs. Chandler was a formidable presence. I was honored to become one of her top lieutenants in the army of volunteers that helped her reach a fund-raising goal in excess of $20 million. I saw firsthand how she could strong-arm the biggest men in the city to donate an amount she decided was appropriate to their wealth. She tore up Kirk's check for $10,000 and told him he could do better. He more than doubled his contribution without a murmur.

Buff wielded enormous power at the LA *Times*. She initiated the annual selection of a *Times* Woman of the Year, an honor I received in 1969. I was her friend until she passed in her Hancock Park mansion in 1997, with me holding her hand.

I met Mrs. Chandler, of course, through Anita May. There were five of us in Anita's favored circle of young wives: Edie Wasserman, Nancy Reagan, Harriet Deutsch, Sara Briskin, and me. We became her protégées. She advised us on clothes, china, and decor—even how to handle our husbands. She was so generous we could never admire something without having the butler hand it to us nicely wrapped when we left. Anita had the best jewelry. I remember a dazzling twenty-carat blue-white diamond. She gave the most beautiful parties with an extraordinary mix of interesting people. There were always pots of white orchids in the rooms.

Anita and Tom moved from their estate on Canon Drive into the enormous penthouse atop the newly opened Beverly Hilton Hotel in 1955. They were the first people in Los Angeles to choose such a lifestyle.

Our little quintet of acolytes listened and learned and formed lasting friendships. I think Anita foresaw Ronald Reagan's political future long before he imagined it for himself. She guided Nancy in that direction.

Kirk had known Ronnie as president of the Screen Actors Guild. In those days he was considered so left-wing that some wondered if he was a communist sympathizer. As soon as he married Nancy Davis, whose Chicago-based family were all Republican, he joined the party. Anita approved.

Nancy and I had only one bump in our long friendship. Our sons, Eric and Ron Jr., were friends and schoolmates at the Thomas Dye School. Nancy and I shared carpool duties. We also manned the hot dog booth together at the annual school fairs. Our booth always made the most money because our movie star husbands took the orders. All was fine between the Douglases and Reagans until the afternoon Eric booed the Goldwater bumper sticker on the back of Nancy's car. She immediately banned the boys from playing with each other and demanded I drive over at once and pick up my son. It took quite a while for Nancy to forgive us for raising a juvenile Democrat. She was a true Republican!

When Kirk and I moved into our own large house on Canon, I used William Haines, the former silent movie star who was Anita's favorite decorator, to make it the showplace it became. So did the other girls in our clique. We all adored Billy, who was openly gay and had a wicked wit. He and his partner of fifty years were welcome guests whenever we entertained.

My first large party in the new house was on March 1, 1957. I wrote my mother-in-law about it on March 6:

> **Dear Ma,**
>
> *I haven't written you in a long time, but preparing for a 6-month trip with the baby is quite a chore.*
>
> *First of all, I would like to know how you enjoyed the Person-to-Person show?* [Kirk had sent her the kinescope of our appearance on the show where Edward R. Murrow visited famous people in their homes.]
>
> *Last Friday we had a very big farewell party for "The Viking" at our new house. I had 172 guests, all sit down, for dinner in a beautiful tent. We had an orchestra and Viking decorations, and the last guest left at four o'clock in the morning. I'm still pretty tired from it, but now I have to prepare Kirk for his trip.*
>
> *He leaves Saturday and Peter and I will follow him on the 31st of March. We will not stop longer than just overnight in New York, but on our way home, Ma, I am sure we will stop to see you all—including Peter.*
>
> *In the meanwhile, take good care of yourself, and we will write to you frequently from wherever we are, so we'll keep in touch. Say hello to the family.*
>
> **All our love,**
> **Anne**

KIRK:

Merle Oberon was another of the women who adored Anne. She became Peter's godmother. (Quique Jourdan was Eric's godmother. She and Louis were two of our best friends.)

Kirk and Merle Oberon at her home in Acapulco

Merle spent a lot of time with us when she was in residence in Los Angeles. We, in turn, had wonderful holidays with her and her husband, Bruno Pagliani, in the palace he built for her in Acapulco. After he died, we continued to socialize with her and her much-younger husband, Rob Wolders, who helped her raise her two adopted children.

Like so many of us, Merle, too, had reinvented herself before she became a movie star in England and married Sir Alexander Korda, a Hungarian Jew and the leading force in British cinema. She claimed she was born in Tasmania, but a fire had destroyed all her records. Only a year before she died in Malibu did Merle own up to being from Bombay—an Anglo Indian girl whose family called her Queenie.

In 1985, Michael Korda wrote a *roman à clef* about his famous aunt's early life; it was an instant bestseller. Not only was I glad to learn from Michael's book about Merle's colorful past, I also got a meaty role in the film adaption of *Queenie*, which ran on ABC-TV in 1987.

ANNE:

Edward G. Robinson was another of my mentors. We bonded over my admiration for his superb taste in art. Soon after the war ended, I got a job at the upscale Galerie Rue du Faubourg. I remember the first big sale I made. The gallery owner and I were going to lunch with Anthony Drexel Duke, scion of the fabled Dukes of North Carolina. Suddenly a bicyclist veered in front of Tony's car. He hit him and the police came. I said to Tony: "Give me a hundred dollars. I'll handle this and meet you both at the restaurant."

At the station, the injured cyclist accepted the money and the incident was closed. A grateful Tony asked what he could do to thank me.

"Buy a painting," I suggested, thinking of my commission. He bought our costliest oil—a beautiful Renoir. I used part of my windfall to purchase my own work of art—a painting which currently hangs in our foyer in the *bijou* house on Rexford we bought after the children were grown.

Between our Beverly Hills and Palm Springs properties, we had some lovely gardens and interiors crying out for works of art. Eddie told me he put half his salary aside, even when he was quite poor, for a down payment on a work for his collection. He lived modestly and his paintings were as dear to him as children. Before I acquired anything, I would first show it to Eddie and get his opinion on its quality and price.

KIRK:

I remember one party at Eddie's when Barbara Stanwyck joined Anne and me on the terrace. It was a cool and slightly windy autumn evening. Barbara hadn't been very nice to me when I played her husband in *The Strange Love of Martha Ivers*, but she was a close friend of Frank Sinatra's first wife Nancy, so we saw her at their house every now and then.

She had the kind of bearing that commanded respect. "Buy this girl a fur wrap," she ordered. "Can't you see she's shivering." I came home with it the very next day. Miss Stanwyck was a formidable presence.

ANNE:

Eddie Robinson, of course, had problems during the blacklist. He was never a communist, but he had lots of friends who were fellow travelers. Until he convinced Hedda Hopper, John Wayne, and Ronald Reagan of his "loyalty" he could no longer get work. In order to pay his bills, he even had to part with one of his precious paintings. His real tragedy came later on, when he finally divorced the terrible woman he had married. She won half the art in the settlement. He tried to buy it back from her at an exorbitant price, but she refused. She sold it off to others to spite him, because she knew that every piece was a part of his heart.

KIRK:

I was never a big gambler, except on my own career. But part of our social life in Los Angeles and Palm Springs revolved around our regular poker games. In Los Angeles we would gather at Janet Leigh's house. After her divorce from Tony Curtis (I was his best man when he married his next wife, Christine Kaufmann), she married Robert Brandt, a successful stockbroker who helped raise the two Curtis daughters. They were very happy and were married until Janet's death in 2004.

Anne and I remained friends with Janet and Tony, and their subsequent mates, till the end of their lives.

ANNE:

I was never sure if Janet married Tony because they were very much in love or because Lew Wasserman pushed them toward it. He was very taken with Janet, but, of course, he was married to Edie. He promoted Tony's career at Universal and then arranged for them to date.

The other regulars in our poker game were Ray and Fran Stark, Lew and Edie Wasserman, and Claire Trevor and her husband, Milton Bren, a former agent and producer of the *Topper* movies, who developed the Sunset Strip. Claire raised his two sons along with her own, and sometimes she would bring her stepson Donald, Chairman of the Irvine Company, to the games, as well as his brother, Peter, if he and his wife happened to be visiting from New York.

All of our friends had one thing in common: they could laugh at themselves and one another. Ray Stark, in particular, was known for his practical jokes. Here's one he played on Irving Lazar, the agent who later became known for his Oscar parties at Wolfgang Puck's original Spago restaurant on Sunset:

With all of us listening, Ray telephoned Irving and pretended to be Gary Cooper. "Would you like to be my exclusive representative?" he asked.

"Of course," Irving replied, salivating almost audibly on the other end of the phone.

"By the way, are you Jewish?" Ray asked.

Irving paused and said: "Not necessarily."

Kirk presents Lifetime Achievement Oscar to Ray Stark in 1980

KIRK:

Our gin rummy pals in Palm Springs were mostly our neighbors on Via Lola in Las Palmas, the small enclave nestled against the San Gabriel Mountains known as the "movie colony." There were Jack and Mary Benny, Gregory and Veronique Peck, Sidney and Alexandra Sheldon, Jules and Doris Stein. For years, we would gather at one of our houses on New Year's Eve for a marathon evening of gin rummy.

During and after the Reagan presidency, however, Anne and I gave up our gin rummy tradition to attend the Annenbergs' grand New Year's Eve parties at their Sunnylands estate. I think Anne and I were the only registered Democrats on the guest list. Anne was invariably seated next to President Reagan, who was very fond of her. Besides, he could rely on her to discreetly whisper to him anything he missed because of his impaired hearing.

Like our friend Dean Martin, I was famous for leaving parties early—even when I was the host. I never went as far as Dean, who once ended a gathering at his place by calling in a noise complaint to the police from his bedroom.

So many of us belied the personas we had with our fans. Dean was far from a heavy drinker; Frank Sinatra didn't hang out with the members of his so-called "Rat Pack" when they weren't working together; Burt Lancaster and I rarely socialized except when it was called for. My friends included Henry Kissinger, Jack Valenti, and various members of the Kennedy clan. Anne was close to the fashion designer Mollie Parnis, who dressed Lady Bird Johnson and other presidential wives and attracted the same level of prominent guests in New York as Anita May did in Los Angeles. Anne would often stay with Mollie at her elegant Park Avenue flat while I was away on location. There, too, Anne joined in gin rummy marathons with Mollie's pals, among them Billy Rose's wife, Bern, and Dr. Mathilde Krim, who became so prominent in the fight against AIDS, partnered with Elizabeth Taylor.

ANNE:

When our friends came to houseguest with us in Palm Springs, I would usually arrange a dinner party in their honor. Truman Capote didn't stay with us, but I invited him to a dinner for twelve when he was visiting someone else. He arrived with a strange young man none of us knew. It turned out Truman didn't know him either.

He worked at the gas station up the road, and Truman said, "Would you like to have dinner with me?" The guy hopped into the car. Truman loved to shock.

My maid Myrtle, a dancer in vaudeville in her youth, also intrigued him. Truman loved her stories about her show-biz days in Harlem and on the circuit. He sent Myrtle a plane ticket to New York and invited her to stay with him for a few days.

On her arrival, he announced he was throwing a luncheon in her honor at the swank Colony Club for his friends to meet her. Of course, he was talking about the beautiful socialites like Babe Paley, Lee Radziwill, and C. Z. Guest, whom he called his swans. Myrtle was mortified. She didn't have a proper outfit, she protested, so Truman took her shopping.

Truman had a vicious, vicious sense of humor. It titillated him to do shocking things; but, of course, it all backfired when he wrote about his swans in *Unanswered Prayers* and they dropped him.

KIRK:

Frank Sinatra held a special place in all of our hearts. He held court at the "Compound" in Rancho Mirage. He moved there after his divorce from Ava Gardner in 1957. They had lived together at Twin Palms, the house in the movie colony of Palm Springs with the grand piano–shaped pool, where we would drop in for cocktails as soon as he hoisted the flag with the Jack Daniels symbol. The Compound was his main residence until his death, although he also lived in Beverly Hills.

Frank had an entourage of old friends—none of them in show business—who hung around him. They would wait home every afternoon to see if Vi, Frank's housekeeper, would call to invite them to dinner.

ANNE:

There was Danny Schwartz, who made a lot of money building low-cost houses in Las Vegas for casino workers, financed initially with a $30,000 loan from Frank. Danny and his wife, Natalie, lived next to the Compound across the golf course from where Zeppo Marx and his wife, Barbara, lived. And, of course, there was Jilly Rizzo, who was sort of Frank's bodyguard.

Zeppo had no other interests than playing golf and playing hearts, and pretty soon Barbara caught Frank's eye. She divorced Zeppo and became Frank's lady. However, he didn't want to get married again, and they broke up. Both of them were obviously unhappy apart, so I decided to do the unheard of. I called Frank and told him he was being foolish. Barbara was a perfect wife for him. She had been a showgirl in Las Vegas and enjoyed his lifestyle. Kirk told me not to interfere, because Frank could be quick to anger. But Frank and I had a special relationship. He called me Frenchie, and would come to the house and cook big Italian meals for me on my birthday. Kirk was his sous-chef. He called Kirk Spartacus.

Frank took my advice, and Barbara Marx became Barbara Sinatra in 1976. There was a big prewedding reception at Melvyn's Restaurant, one of his favorite hangouts, the night before. Everybody came to our house to dress for the wedding, including Sidney Korshak, the well-connected lawyer who handled a lot of business for both movie moguls and mobsters, and his wife, Bea, who had decorated the main house of the Compound in Frank's favorite color, orange. After arriving, Sidney said to me, "It would be great if Bea and I could live on this street."

"There just happens to be a very nice house for sale a few doors down," I told him. He asked the price. "I think they are asking $45,000."

Sidney made the owners an offer of $30,000 before we headed off to the wedding ceremony at Sunnylands. By the time we got back, Sidney had finalized the deal for $35,000 and we had new neighbors.

KIRK:

When I was still a theater actor in New York, I was irritated at this Frank Sinatra, whose fans snarled traffic in front of the Paramount Theater every night, making it hard for me to get home to Greenwich Village. But we became good friends in Hollywood, and when my recording of "Whale of a Tale" topped his latest single on the *Billboard* charts, I lorded it over him.

In 1956, we were competing for the title role in *Pal Joey*. This was right after Frank won the Oscar for his stunning dramatic performance in *From Here to Eternity*. My agent let me know that Sinatra had been given the part, and I sent him this note on February 20, 1956:

> *Dear Frankie,*
> *What are you trying to get—bookends? I'm a little jealous, but congratulations.*
>
> *Sincerely,*
> *Kirk*

February 20, 1956

Dear Frankie,

    What are you trying to get --
bookends?

    I'm a little jealous, but con-
gratulations.

Mr. Frank Sinatra
10372½ Wilshire Blv
Beverly Hills, Cal:

COLUMBIA PICTURES CORPORATION

OFFICE OF THE
PRESIDENT

1438 NO. GOWER STREET
HOLLYWOOD 28, CALIFORNIA

March 14
19   56

Dear Kirk:

The way our script of PAL JOEY is developing, with
emphasis on the singing and musical elements, the
role of "Joey" does not seem as suitable to you as
was contemplated when we discussed the picture.

We were obliged, therefore, to think in terms of
a singer-actor like Frank Sinatra and change our
production plans until his availability, which
will be in the early part of next year.

I want to express my appreciation to you for the
consideration and courtesies you gave us in this
and on other subjects. And I hope that we will
find an important project soon which will be good
for you and which you will want to do.

My cordial regards to you.

Sincerely,

HARRY COHN

HC
jw

Mr. Kirk Douglas
% Mr. Harold Ro
Famous Ar

On March 14, 1956, Harry Cohn, the president of Columbia Pictures, wrote me this letter. It was unusual, I was told, for him to explain a casting decision to an actor. Of course, it wasn't news. The columns had written about it weeks before.

> **Dear Kirk:**
>
> *The way our script of* Pal Joey *is developing, with emphasis on the singing and musical elements, the role of* Joey *does not seem as suitable to you as was contemplated when we discussed the picture.*
>
> *We were obliged, therefore, to think in terms of a singer-actor like Frank Sinatra and change our production plans until his availability, which will be in the early part of next year.*
>
> *I want to express my appreciation to you for the consideration and courtesies you gave us in this and on other subjects. And I hope that we will find an important project soon which will be good for you and which you will want to do.*
>
>

My cordial regards to you.
Sincerely,
Harry Cohn
>

ANNE:

I don't think Frank ever got over the hurt of President Kennedy's rejection. He had worked so hard to get JFK elected and expected him to visit the Compound often. He made sure the Secret Service would find it a secure location with sufficient accommodations for the president's needs. After Bobby convinced his brother that staying there was a detriment because of Frank's suspected mob ties, Frank became an ardent Republican. However, he remained liberal to the core in his dedication to righteous causes, and was particularly partial to Jews and Israel.

KIRK:

Sinatra and I were the kind of friends who would always go the extra mile for each other. I miss him. He had an intelligence and grace that added so much to my life. It was an honor and a privilege to give a eulogy at his funeral.

When Frank tried to get a casino license in 1981, he asked Gregory Peck and me to speak on his behalf before the Board. This is the letter of thanks I got:

February 12, 1981

Dear Kirk:

I don't want to let the moment of the Vegas hearing go by without expressing my love and gratitude to you for stepping out of the crowd on my behalf.

Hopefully this hearing has ended the parade of abuse that has been marching through my life for these past years. If so, I owe much of the peace ahead to you.

I pray the good Lord will bless you and keep you forever in his heart. And that you'll always keep my number handy. No matter what the need, I'll be there.

I appreciate your faith in me. I hope you know it was not misplaced.

I love you,
Francis Albert

I have a number of other letters from Old Blue Eyes that I treasure equally. For a man who never had the benefit of a college education, I consider Frank to be one of the most eloquent and intelligent communicators I have ever known. I will share just a couple more:

FRANK SINATRA

December, 1982

Dear Kirk,

Received an invitation to attend your being
honored by the Israel Institute of Technology.
I am delighted they've chosen you because
you are one of the world's great scientists.
Einstein would have envied you with your
knowledge of aerodynamics, nuclear energy, etc.
etc. etc.

Naturally I would have attended if I were not
working in Vegas to make a pot of money.
However, if I could have attended, noting in
the invitation that Barbara Walters is the
guest speaker, I would have brought a translator
with me.

I send Anne,the woman who is your wife, hugs
and kisses; for you, nothing!

Francis Albert

PS - My love to Mother Lancaster

Mr. K
805 N
Bever.

FS:d

March 30, 1978

Dear Izzy:

1. I read the script as soon as I received it.

2. I got the flu and had it for four weeks.

3. Packed my bags and went on the road.

4. I reread the script.

5. I finally got around to writing you about it.

6. The script is fun but it's not really anything I want to play.

7. I'm on my way to Israel.

8. Sorry you couldn't be with us.

9. Barbara sends love to you and Annie as do I.

10. Goodbye.

Francis Albert

December, 1982

Dear Kirk,

Received an invitation to attend your being honored by the Israel Institute of Technology. I am delighted they've chosen you because you are one of the world's great scientists. Einstein would have envied you with your knowledge of aerodynamics, nuclear energy, etc. etc. etc.

Naturally I would have attended if I were not working in Vegas to make a pot of money. However, if I could have attended, noting in the invitation that Barbara Walters is the guest speaker, I would have brought a translator with me.

I send Anne, the woman who is your wife, hugs and kisses; for you, nothing!

Francis Albert

P.S. My love to Mother Lancaster

OPPOSITE: *Master chef Sinatra and sous-chef Kirk prepare Anne's birthday dinner*

CHAPTER TEN

A Life Beyond Hollywood

ANNE:

When Senator John Fitzgerald Kennedy defeated Vice President Richard Milhous Nixon for the presidency in November 1960, we were all giddy with hope for the new decade. We first met JFK during a party at Charlie Feldman's house soon after Kirk and I were married. Charlie was the überagent who created Famous Artists; Ray Stark worked there. Charlie pointed Kennedy out and said, "He's going to be president of the United States."

KIRK:

I certainly knew he'd get the women's votes, because all the ladies at Charlie's were gravitating in his direction. He had more charisma than all of us movie stars put together.

But, then, politics is a performance art, too. There's always been synergy between Hollywood and Washington. The lines between our worlds of make-believe and reality often blur—sometimes in the most bizarre ways. The motivation of John Hinckley Jr., the would-be assassin of President Reagan, wasn't political. He just wanted to impress Jodie Foster, whom he'd been obsessed with since seeing her in *Taxi Driver*. Ironically, he chose the one president who came out of the film industry.

I don't know what in human nature makes people care about what famous people do, what they think, and what befalls them, but those of us who fall into that category seem to inspire insatiable curiosity from the public.

Jack Kennedy knew and understood the phenomenon and used it to his advantage. In my opinion, he—not Ronald Reagan—was our first movie star president. But then, his family had had a toe in the film business ever since Joseph P. Kennedy Sr. refinanced three studios and combined them into RKO. While the old man had dabbled in Hollywood romances (primarily, it is said, with Gloria Swanson), he now had a daughter married to a movie star and two married sons who were gossiped about for supposed liaisons with Marilyn Monroe.

ANNE:

I met Patricia Kennedy Lawford, Peter's wife, through the playwright and Oscar-winning screenwriter Lenny Gershe. He took me to a luncheon at the Lawford beach house in the summer of 1960, just before the start of the Democratic Convention in Los Angeles. Pat seated me next to her father, and I committed an instant *faux pas* when I reminded Mr. Kennedy we had met before in Paris at the races. I mentioned the well-known *demimondaine* beauty who accompanied him. Now that his son was running for the highest office in the land, the Kennedys were trying to downplay their racy reputations.

Pat introduced us to Bobby and Ethel, and they became great pals of ours. None of us could have imagined the great tragedies that lay ahead for this tight-knit clan which was so much fun to be around.

KIRK:

I wrote President Kennedy this letter the first week of 1963 in response to one he had sent me. This is what I said:

> ### Dear Mr. President:
> *I certainly appreciate your taking the time to write me a note of thanks for the narration that I did on the picture,* An Answer.
> *I feel that, more and more, you instill in the American people the feeling that they must "ask not what your country*

*can do for you—ask what you can do for your country." In
my opinion, this is the strongest way that we can give thanks
for a way of life that enables us to attain here what we could
not get under another system.*

*I also feel that you've succeeded in making people proud
to be called upon to do something for our country—no matter
how small. I'm happy to be asked to participate in the Inaugural celebration on January 18th.*

*May God give you health and wisdom to cope with any
problems that may lie ahead.*

Sincerely,
Kirk Douglas

My role at the Second Inaugural Anniversary Salute was to be Master
of Ceremonies with Gene Kelly. We assembled a stunning program with
performances by George Burns; Carol Channing; Carol Burnett; Shirley
Bassey; Diahann Carroll; Yves Montand; opera diva Joan Sutherland; the
folk trio Peter, Paul and Mary; and both the Flamenco Ballet and the
New York City Ballet featuring Arthur Mitchell. While Washington still
had segregated restrooms and drinking fountains, this Inaugural Salute
was fully integrated and international. Before our Inaugural Salute at
the National Guard Armory, President and Mrs. Kennedy attended the
$1,000 a plate dinner at the International Inn. The Gala tickets were
only $100, with no food. The two sellout events wiped out the large debt
the Democratic Party was carrying.

ANNE:

While Kirk and Gene were getting ready, I was at the pricey dinner
with Carroll Rosenbloom, the owner of the Los Angeles Rams foot-
ball team.

It's hard to describe my feelings, both as a woman and as a natu-
ralized American, when JFK stopped by our table. With his blue eyes
twinkling, the president shook my hand and said, "Aren't you with the
wrong guy?"

It had been a rainy day in Washington, which turned into an icy deluge that was expected to last the weekend. The airports were shut down, stranding us for a few extra days in the nation's capital. Ethel Kennedy suggested Kirk and I round up some of the others from the show and come to dinner the following day. We had a merry meal at their estate, Hickory Hill, with Gene Kelly, George Burns, the Tom Bradens, Carol Channing and her husband, our hosts Bobby and Ethel and the Ted Kennedys. Then we all trooped off to the White House in a small convoy of station wagons.

KIRK:

The president and first lady had been scheduled for a weekend at Camp David with their good friends, British Ambassador Sir David Ormsby-Gore and his wife. The weather changed their plans, too.

In the movie business, we expect the unexpected. But this unexpected invitation from the president of the United States topped any others in my life. I think Anne will agree.

ANNE:

There we were, sitting on the floor in the living room of the first family's private quarters—cracking jokes, drinking, and almost everyone but me giving impromptu performances. The president poured champagne into Jackie's shoe and drank from it. Joan Kennedy went to the piano and played as Ted sang something rousing. Carol Channing sang "Diamonds Are a Girl's Best Friend," George Burns did one of his routines, and Kirk sang a raucous "I'm Red Hot Henry Brown, the Hottest Man in Town." The president sat in his famous rocking chair and gave Kirk a thumbs-up. Then, not to be outdone, Bobby and he got up together and sang, almost in a monotone, a camp song they learned as kids.

KIRK:

After that, Jackie offered to take the ladies on a tour of the private quarters, and off they went. We men remained with the president, who

KIRK DOUGLAS

707 North Canon Drive
Beverly Hills, California

January 4, 1963

Dear Mr. President:

I certainly appreciate your taking the time to write me a note of thanks for the narration that I did on the picture, An Answer.

I feel that, more and more, you instill in the American people the feeling that they must "ask not what your country can do for you -- ask what you can do for your country." In my opinion, this is the strongest way that we can give thanks for a way of life that enables us to attain here what we could not get under another system.

I also feel that you've succeeded in making people proud to be called upon to do something for our country -- no matter how small. I'm happy to be asked to participate in the inaugural celebration on January 18th.

May God give you health and wisdom to cope with any problems that may lie ahead.

Sincerely,

Kirk Douglas

President John F. Kennedy
The White House
Washington, D. C.

offered us cigars from the private stash of Cubans David Ormsby-Gore smuggled in for him in his diplomatic pouch. I had stopped smoking years before, but this was a special occasion.

Just after Jackie and the ladies took off, the president looked at me in great amusement: "I wonder if Jackie remembers that my mother is in the Lincoln bedroom?"

ANNE:

We were all curious to see what passed for normal life in the White House and how Jackie had decorated their quarters. When we came to the Lincoln bedroom, Jackie knocked lightly and opened the door. Rose Kennedy was in bed reading a book. We were all embarrassed to intrude on her, but she acted as if this was nothing out of the ordinary. I guess with that many high-spirited children, nothing could faze her. A few years later Kirk and I were sleeping in that same bedroom as guests of President and Lady Bird Johnson.

Sir David and his wife were charming, but the next time we saw them was not such a happy occasion. It was June 6, 1968, at St. Patrick's Cathedral in New York. The ambassador was no longer in public life, having assumed the title and duties of Lord Harlech when his father died. He was a pallbearer at Bobby's funeral, the second of his Kennedy friends to fall to an assassin's bullet. Afterward, we all boarded the train bearing Bobby's body to Arlington Cemetery.

KIRK:

When I was in Washington to meet with the authors of *Seven Days in May*, I went to Vice President Johnson's home for a buffet lunch. As I was standing with my empty plate, President Kennedy got in line behind me.

"Are you going to make a film of *Seven Days in May*?" he asked.

The Pentagon had already weighed in with their disapproval of the book and any plans for a movie. "Not if you don't want me to," I answered. I hadn't yet finalized my deal for the rights.

The president spent the next twenty minutes explaining to me with great enthusiasm just why I had to do it. I'm glad I listened to him.

We filmed most of *Seven Days in May* in California: in the studio, in Lake Arrowhead and in San Diego; we did have to go to Washington briefly to get a shot in front of the White House, and one of me going in and out of the Pentagon. I called JFK. He went to Hyannis Port for a couple of days so I could film without interference from the Secret Service. We then "stole" the Pentagon footage by concealing a camera that caught me walking up the stairs in my colonel's uniform, exchanging salutes with a lower-ranking officer, going inside, and walking out again. It seems no one can tell the difference between a movie colonel and a real one!

As summer progressed in 1963, Ethel and Bobby added still another baby to their brood. Anne and I received this note from Ethel, who was at the Compound in Hyannis Port. She had the best sense of humor, and I have many examples of our witty exchanges.

> **Dear Anne and Kirk,**
>
> *Such a happy thank you for your wonderful telegram. It was great of you to think of us. Christopher is adjusting rapidly to his family's hectic life and all of the other children adore him, especially Kerry, who is just the right age to enjoy a baby brother.*
>
> *Anne was magnificent in the PT 109 TV show. We couldn't see the guy who was with her—Eunice kept running up to the screen and kissing him.*
>
> **Xxx & ooo's, Ethel**

ANNE:

President Kennedy suggested that Kirk visit foreign countries to talk with world leaders and their people about America. He understood that movie stars had fame and fans all over the world. My Spartacus could win new friends for the United States even in communist countries and dictatorships. Kirk wanted me to join him on these missions, because I had fluency in four languages; I also spoke passable Spanish after all our trips to Mexico. He also relied on my knowledge of protocol, honed by my work at the Cannes Film Festival.

We started in Colombia in 1962 and on another occasion we went to Berlin. That was interesting to me to be in a city, now divided, I had known so well from staying with my mother. We spent time in both parts of the city. All was optimism and hope in West Berlin but things were different on the other side of Checkpoint Charlie. We went to East Berlin because all of the great cultural institutions were on that side of the wall—the museums, the Philharmonic, the theaters.

We were given a tour of two enormous hotels built by Canadians. They were open for business, but we saw no guests. In the cavernous presidential suite with bedrooms, dining rooms, living rooms, and office space, there was a small sparsely furnished room—just two plain chairs and a table. I asked our genial government guide, "What is this room for?"

"This is the room where you sit and think about how you pay for the hotel bill," he quipped. I thought that, more likely, it was used to eavesdrop on influential foreigners and record their conversations.

KIRK:

Under President Johnson, I formalized with the State Department's USIA (United States Information Agency) my position as a goodwill ambassador. I asked for two things in return: that Anne be considered an equal partner and that I be allowed to pay for everything myself. I didn't think it right to use taxpayer money. Together, we visited more than forty countries over the next decades, under both Democratic and Republican presidents. President Carter awarded me the Medal of Freedom and Anne received the Director's Award from the State Department for increasing international understanding. I would attend briefings in Washington before each trip, and submit written reports on my return.

ANNE:

No matter how successful Kirk was as a film actor and producer, no matter how at home he was in the White House and embassies abroad, he still felt a failure because he hadn't conquered Broadway. It was an itch

Students at a Japanese university attend Kirk's lecture on America

that needed to be scratched.

When he read Ken Kesey's debut novel, *One Flew Over the Cuckoo's Nest*, he saw its dramatic possibilities and acquired the rights. Dale Wasserman—who wrote the first draft screenplay of *The Vikings*—wrote the stage adaptation. A few years later, Dale had a major hit with *Man of La Mancha*.

With *Seven Days in May* in postproduction, Kirk felt free to go to New York where he assembled a first-rate cast for *One Flew Over the Cuckoo's Nest*: Gene Wilder, Ed Ames, William Daniels, and Joan Tetzel. After brilliant out-of-town reviews, opening night was set for November 13, 1963, on Broadway.

As usual, I was at home in Beverly Hills, taking care of business and the children. I sent this letter to Kirk at the Hampshire House in Manhattan.

Wednesday, October 16, 11 p.m.

Mon Amour,

I am a little afraid to write this letter because "sloppy as you are," you are likely going to leave this valuable compromising document lying around for anybody to read!

I hope you are as nervous as I am as the days come closer for the opening. They say it is a good sign to be nervous—well if it is to judge by me—it will be a smash—I am a wreck! I feel so for you but I have to remind myself that it is your guts and not mine that you use to get out there in front of that cruel world.

I am so proud of you. I cannot tell you enough. I know and understand what it means for you to go back to Broadway and give it another try. Darling, you can do no wrong with your decision—regardless of the outcome. I love you very deeply and I love our children. I am grateful for the wonderful lives that we are having thanks to your talent. We must realize that we really have everything—we don't need anything more—everything "more" is an extra!

Now if I were you, I would put this letter away somewhere safe—and each time I am nasty to you—shove it under my nose!!

[Signed with a heart] *Stolz*

I flew to New York a few days before opening night. Kirk scribbled this note and sent it over to me at the Hampshire House a couple of hours before the curtain went up.

My darling—

No matter what happens tonight I love you. And please know how much I appreciate your patience at my unreasonable attitude.—Boy if I were you I certainly wouldn't want to be married to me—But Thank God you're you and thank God I've got you.

Tonight I "walk a picket fence for you"! I'm showing off for you and if I fall down, I'll know you still love me. But I

Anne and Kirk, 1979

am going to try to be a success for you and Peter and Eric. For you especially because I love you—for the kids so that when they grow up they'll know that their old man had guts and he "tried—goddamit, I tried."

Tonight, have fun, I'll be over my nerves and I'll be giving a show for <u>you</u>—as to the rest—Fug 'em all!—

I love you—
K

KIRK:

Well, after the glowing reviews in Boston, what a rude shock. The New York critics were brutal. They missed the point of the whole play and even accused us of making fun of mental patients. Then, just nine days later, the whole country was a madhouse.

I was in a cab heading for the theater on Friday afternoon, November 22. Suddenly the driver swerved to the curb. With tears in his eyes, he told me the news that had just come over the radio. President Kennedy had been pronounced dead after being shot in Dallas. Lyndon Johnson would be sworn in on Air Force One as our new president. We went through the motions of the performance as if this were a normal night, but it felt like all the air had gone out of the world.

Everyone of a certain age can tell you exactly where they were and what they were doing when they heard that President Kennedy had been shot. Years later, the Soviet poet Yevgeny Yevtushenko told me Russians were crying in the street.

ANNE:

I was flying back to Los Angeles, and there was no announcement on the plane. The nanny and the kids were at the airport to meet me. She broke the news: "President Kennedy was assassinated in Dallas. He is dead."

I was numb. I called Lenny Gershe as soon as I got in the house. He said, "I'll be there in half an hour. We are going out to be with Pat."

We arrived to find the house surrounded by Secret Service. Pat and Peter had separated by this time, so we stayed with her until she was escorted to the airport. I felt horrible to think of her all alone on that plane, accompanied only by a few press people who were covering the tragedy.

KIRK:

I kept the show running for five months. It was heavily in the red. I tried to buy some more time by cutting salaries, but the cast wouldn't hear of it. I posted the closing notice and our final performance was January 25, 1964. Ironically, that was also the day of our first sneak preview of *Seven*

Days in May. I stopped by the theater as the lights came up. When the audience saw me, they gave me a standing ovation. I felt like God was telling me it was okay to just be a movie star.

The day before, I had received the letter Tony Curtis wrote on January 20. He was expecting to see me when he got to New York the following week. By then, I was back in L.A.

Dear Kirk:

A little time has passed now and you have kind of settled into the play. I hope you're well physically and emotionally. I think you have done a terrific job fighting with those pricks in New York—I am, of course, referring to the critics.

I had a gag planned to send you the day after your opening in New York, but when I heard of the reviews, I didn't think the joke would work properly, so I decided against it. I am not going to tell you in a letter what it was, but will tell you when I see you in New York.

I've been very busy. I'm just finishing Sex and the Single Girl, *which I did with Natalie Wood, and getting ready to do a picture at Fox the middle of March. . . .*

We haven't seen Anne, but every now and then I hear she's in town or on her way to New York. We've been rather lax in getting in touch with her, but we really haven't done anything, Kirk. Christina is pregnant. . . . We haven't been out at all and haven't missed anybody, with the exception of you and one or two others.

I won't bore you with a long letter—just wanted to let you know we'll see you in a week or so in New York. Christina joins me in our affection to you.

Tony

TONY CURTIS

January 20
1 9 6 4

Dear Kirk:

A little time has passed now and you have kind of
settled into the play. I hope you're well physically
and emotionally. I think you have done a terrific
job fighting with those pricks in New York - I am,
of course, referring to the critics.

I had a gag planned to send you the day after your
opening in New York, but when I heard of the reviews,
I didn't think the joke would work properly, so I
decided against it. I am not going to tell you in
a letter what it was, but will tell you when I see
you in New York.

I've been very busy. I'm just finishing SEX AND THE
SINGLE GIRL, which I did with Natalie Wood, and
getting ready to do a picture at Fox the middle of
March. Incidentally, we're going to be in New York
in about a week, staying at the St. Regis, and I'll
call you as soon as we arrive.

Everything has been very quiet here. The weather has
been fabulous, but I must say I am looking forward to
going back East and getting some nippy weather. We
haven't seen Anne, but every now and then I hear she's
in town or on her way to New York. We've been rather
lax in getting in touch with her, but we really haven't
done anything, Kirk. Christina is pregnant and we've
really done nothing, except go to a few screenings.
We haven't been out at all and haven't missed anybody,
with the exception of you and one or two others. Other
than that, there's no one you want to spend time with.

I won't bore you with a long letter - just wanted to
let you know we'll see you in a week or so in New York.
Christina joins me in our affection to you.

Tony

The Great White Way and I remained disappointed lovers. I only performed onstage twice more: a six-week run in San Francisco with Burt Lancaster in *The Boys of Autumn,* a two-hander about the later years of Huck Finn and Tom Sawyer (it flopped on Broadway with a different cast), and my one-man show, *Before I Forget,* which I performed on two weekends in 2008, when I was only ninety-two at the Culver City theater that bears my name—not because of my fame, but because Anne and I gave the Center Theatre Group of the Music Center several million dollars to turn the defunct Art Deco Theatre near the old MGM studio into a modern performing space.

As for *One Flew Over the Cuckoo's Nest,* I am happy I lived to see tastes change. My son Michael turned it into a hit film with my blessing in 1975, after I struggled for more than ten years to pull a production together. In 2001, it was a big hit on Broadway at last, winning the Tony for Best Play Revival. Gary Sinise played my role. I sent him this note of congratulations:

> **Dear Gary,**
> *I'm very happy for you and your "crew" for getting the Tony, you deserve it! How lucky for you that you did not see my performance years ago. Jack Nicholson didn't see it either, and you both won awards!*
>
> > **All my best,**
> > **Kirk**

———————| ★ |———————

ANNE:

So Kirk came home and made more pictures, sandwiched between a few multicountry trips on several continents for the USIA. We met kings and queens in Greece and Thailand. We met dictators in Eastern Europe, like Romanian President Nicolae Ceaușescu and his wife, Elena, (who were executed by firing squad after a revolution), and Marshal Tito, the president of Yugoslavia, who adored movie stars and entertained us at the opulent summer residence on Brijuni Island.

Just as President Kennedy had predicted, as a movie star, Kirk was a big hit everywhere we went. He was a perfect ambassador to explain American values and attitudes. I was as proud of him as I was of my adopted country.

KIRK:

This reminds me of an experience I had in Yugoslavia. I found myself in the same elevator as the British Ambassador, who was amazed that Anne and I had been personal guests of President Tito.

"Tell me your secret," he said. "I've been waiting to present my credentials to him for nearly six months."

"How many films have you made, Mr. Ambassador?" I replied.

In 1983, I went to Pakistan without Anne to visit the overflowing Afghan refugee camps. Afghanistan had been invaded by Russia, and we were very concerned about its displaced people. My visit got tremendous press coverage in Pakistan and elsewhere. We made a documentary that played all over the world and I had cordial meetings with President Zia. Back in the United States, I wrote impassioned op-ed pieces and held a press conference, never dreaming that we ourselves would get bogged down in a seemingly hopeless war in Afghanistan within another couple of decades.

Here's a letter I received from the deputy director of the USIA about my activities, dated February 18, 1983.

> *Dear Kirk:*
>
> *You already know from the tremendous response in this country and abroad that your visit to the Afghan refugees and your informed comments on their situation and on Soviet activities in Afghanistan had a remarkable effect on international opinion.*
>
> *A recent telegram from our post in Moscow notes that* Sovetskaya Rossiya *carried a story February 6 on your visit*

Office of the Director

USIA

February 18, 1983

Dear Kirk:

You already know from the tremendous response in this country
and abroad that your visit to the Afghan refugees and your
informed comments on their situation and on Soviet activities
in Afghanistan had a remarkable effect on international
opinion.

A recent telegram from our post in Moscow notes that <u>Sovetskaya
Russiya</u> carried a story February 6 on your visit and your
Washington press conference. The article is complimentary to
you as an artist, but criticizes you for "roving the world at
the behest of the State Department and USIA," so t____
there is a crisis, there is also ___

According to <u>Sovetskaya</u> ___
their homeland of their ___
hatred of the people's r___
bandit scum" under your ___

The story concludes that ___
manipulate (your) popular___
do not want peace and mut___

The notice that the Soviet___
on behalf of Afghanistan i___
effectiveness in the cause___

With gratitude and best re___

Mr. Kirk Douglas
305 North Rexford Drive
Beverly Hills, California 912___

*Pakistani newspaper
coverage of Kirk's
visit to an Afghan
refugee camp*

wartzstein in un'intervista al nostro giornale

UCCIDE MIGLIAIA DI INNOCE

and your Washington press conference. The article is complimentary to you as an artist, but criticizes you for "roving the
world at the behest of the State Department and USIA," so
that "where there is a crisis, there is also a star."

According to Sovetskaya Rossiya, the Afghan refugees "left
their homeland of their own free will because of their blind
hatred of the people's revolution," and you have taken "these
bandit scum" under your wing.

The story concludes that you do not "see that those who
manipulate (your) popularity and unscrupulous political
goals do not want peace and 'mutual understanding.'"

The notice that the Soviet press has given to your activities
on behalf of Afghanistan is the best evidence yet of your great
effectiveness in the cause of Afghanistan and of freedom.

With gratitude and best regards.

Sincerely,
Gilbert A. Robinson
Deputy Director

CHAPTER ELEVEN

Friends in High Places

KIRK:

I admired Lyndon Johnson for his leadership in the aftermath of the Kennedy assassination. I don't think anyone but LBJ, with his deep knowledge of how Washington worked, could have conducted the nation's business so ably at that time.

Both Vice President Johnson and the political consultant Jack Valenti were in the motorcade on November 22, 1963. The lives of these two Texans changed forever the moment President Kennedy died. In the historic photo of the swearing-in on Air Force One, Jack's stunned face is visible on the far left. LBJ brought him along to Washington to be his special assistant and made him live in the White House for the first several months. Jack spent so much time in the Oval Office that he fell in love with the president's personal secretary, Mary Margaret.

In 1966, Lew Wasserman told Lyndon he was co-opting Jack to run the newly formed Motion Picture Association of America (MPAA), a lobby group for the top studios. Even the president couldn't say no to Lew, the most powerful Democratic fund-raiser on the west coast. Jack still headquartered in Washington, but he and Mary Margaret spent a lot of time in Hollywood. For more than forty-five years, he was my closest friend.

ANNE:

When Kirk went to Washington for USIA meetings, Jack would take him to the West Wing to visit with the president. I, however, became close to the Johnsons through our mutual friend, Mollie Parnis. They adored her. The president for me was like a big teddy bear, slightly unkempt, radiating energy. He was a little rough around the edges but everybody we met on our trips abroad really liked him. He was very kind and he adored his daughters.

Arthur Krim and his wife, Mathilde, owned a getaway spread near the LBJ ranch in Stonewall, Texas. They would drive over when we house-guested with the Johnsons and sometimes Mollie would join us from New York. Succeeding the glamorous Jackie Kennedy was not easy for Lady Bird, and I admired her tremendously. I think she was relieved when Lyndon announced he wouldn't run for reelection in 1968, especially with anti-war protesters marching in the streets to chants of "Hey, hey, LBJ, how many kids did you kill today?" Of course, we all expected Robert F. Kennedy to succeed him.

KIRK:

Over the decades, I have corresponded with all of our presidents from JFK to Barack Obama. Some embraced Anne and me as friends. I often expressed my opinions as a private and concerned citizen. Here's what I wrote to Lyndon Johnson in the early years of his presidency:

June 16, 1964

Dear Mr. President:
. . . During my trip through the Far East for the USIA (India, Thailand, Philippines, Hong Kong, and Japan) I talked— for the most part—to university students. During the question and answer session, I found that one of the things that amazed them the most, was the quick and orderly transition from the tragic death of President Kennedy to your taking over the office.

In each country they seemed so astonished to learn how a democracy was able to cope with such an unforeseen tragedy. Everywhere I went I felt a very favorable attitude of respect and admiration towards you. Needless to say, I share this feeling very strongly.

Now, when our country faces the appalling situation that someone like Goldwater might possibly be one of the candidates for the office of the president of the United States, let's thank God that you will be the other candidate—and the next president.

Sincerely yours,
Kirk Douglas

P.S. My wife and I still have wonderful memories of the delightful reception you and Mrs. Johnson extended to all of us at your home after the second Inaugural Anniversary Salute in 1963. We were honored to be a part of it.

Shortly after the inauguration in 1965, I wrote again:

Dear Mr. President:
Immediately after the election, I did another tour for the USIA, speaking primarily to university students in Yugoslavia, Greece, Turkey, Israel, and Norway. I was fascinated by the tremendous relief that the people in every country had about your landslide victory. Of course, there are many people who do not understand how your opponent was able to garner over twenty-five million votes. Sometimes it is difficult to make them aware that only in a dictatorship are elections won by a 100% Plurality.

It has been most gratifying to see the increased respect and affection for you during the past few months. The culmination of all this took place as a result of your inspired address to Congress in regard to the civil rights program. The president of the United States is not only the leader of our people, he is looked upon as leader to most of the people around the world. I can only hope that your busy schedule will permit you soon to make a visit to Europe and feel for yourself the warmth and admiration that exists for our president.

My deepest wishes for your continued good health and great leadership.

Sincerely,
Kirk Douglas

ANNE:

Like Anita May in Los Angeles and Mollie Parnis in New York, Washington, too, had a favorite hostess—Joan Braden. Close friends of Robert and Ethel Kennedy, Joan and Tom were with us the night we ended up at the White House with JFK and Jackie.

Invitations to Joan's gatherings were coveted by the Who's Who of Washington. Tom had a similar fan club. The Bradens met and married in D.C., but we first met them in California, where Tom owned a newspaper and was a big shot in Democratic politics. They returned to the capital after Bobby's assassination; Tom had been next to him when he was shot.

The Bradens lived in an unpretentious yellow clapboard house in Chevy Chase, Maryland, large enough to accommodate them and their eight kids. (Tom's lighthearted book about the family, called *Eight Is Enough,* was turned into a popular TV sitcom.) In D.C., he became the cohost of *Crossfire* and wrote a syndicated column, and Joan ran the State Department's consumer affairs division.

KIRK:

Anne and I were in awe of Joan's energy and her skills as a hostess. At her gatherings, Democrats and Republicans could relax with each other and mingle with diplomats from all over the globe. Anne and I felt lucky to be included in the mix when we were in town. That's where we first got to know Nelson Rockefeller and Henry Kissinger.

In 1989, Joan wrote a book called *Just Enough Rope: An Intimate Memoir*, which raised more than a few eyebrows. This is what our friend Maureen Dowd of the *New York Times* said about it: "Joan Braden has taken a lot of heat for this book. . . . This reviewer does not take such a harsh view. How can a book be all bad that features a shower scene with Nelson Rockefeller, a bedroom scene with Bobby Kennedy, a toe-tingling lunch with Kirk Douglas and an account of Frank Sinatra singing 'High Hopes' without his toupee?"

ANNE:

The serious Henry Kissinger of the Nixon administration was a far different person when he visited us. In 1971 he told Kirk: "I play on the west coast. I behave myself in Washington." That's the year I introduced Henry to Jill St. John. It was just after she starred as Sean Connery's love interest in *Diamonds Are Forever*. Jill was gorgeous, and she had an IQ of 163. They had a lovely romance before Henry finally settled down in 1974 with Nancy Maginnes, who had been Nelson Rockefeller's long-time aide. This letter shows the humorous Kissinger we knew:

Dear Kirk:

Nancy and I are deeply sorry we cannot be with you tonight to join in honoring you as an old and dear friend. Perhaps one of the reasons I have always felt so close to you is that there seems to be an uncanny parallel between your screen roles and my own life.

Two Week in Another Town could have been about one of my shuttle negotiations.

In Spartacus you were crucified. I know the sensation.

Town without Pity captured the Washington atmosphere completely.

In Gunfight at the O.K. Corral you were the cowboy alone on his horse—an obvious parallel.

In 20,000 Leagues Under the Sea your submarine ran into all sorts of troubles—and believe me, I know what it

HENRY A. KISSINGER

April 15, 1977

Dear Kirk:

Nancy and I are deeply sorry we cannot be with
you tonight to join in honoring you as an old
and dear friend. Perhaps one of the reasons I
have always felt so close to you is that there
seems to be an uncanny parallel between your
screen roles and my own life.

-- Two Weeks in Another Town could have been
about one of my shuttle negotiations.

-- In Spartacus you were crucified. I know
the sensation.

-- Town without Pity captured the Washington
atmosphere completely.

-- In Gunfight at the O.K. Corral you were
the cowboy alone on his horse -- an obvious parallel.

-- In 20,000 Leagues Under the Sea your submarine ran into all sorts of troubles -- and
believe me, I know what it means to have uncontrollable leaks.

-- Top Secret Affair could have been about any
number of my private negotiations.

-- In Lonely are the Brave you played a man
whose world had changed so completely that he no
longer had a place in it -- I was thinking about
that all the way to work on the bus last week.

-- And when they take away my Secret Service
detail, I Walk Alone will be directly appropriate.

But, Kirk, I want you to know that there are few
people I love, admire and respect more. You have

- 2 -

always been a star in the fullest sense, and
Nancy and I drink to you in spirit tonight.
Just be careful what film you decide to do next!

Warm regards,

Henry A. Kissinger

means to have uncontrollable leaks.

Top Secret Affair *could have been about any number of my private negotiations.*

In Lonely are the Brave *you played a man whose world had changed so completely that he no longer had a place in it—I was thinking about that all the way to work on the bus last week.*

And when they take away my Secret Service detail, I Walk Alone *will be directly appropriate.*

But Kirk, I want you to know that there are few people I move, admire and respect more. You have always been a star in the fullest sense, and Nancy and I drink to you in spirit tonight. Just be careful what film you decide to do next!

Warm regards,
Henry A. Kissinger

In 1971 I wrote this to Kirk, who was filming abroad:

Darling, my only love,
I came back from Palm Springs by limo courtesy of Danny Schwartz [one of Sinatra's inner circle]. The weather was terrific—95 degrees during the day and 48 at night!

Sunday we had a very nice lunch around the pool with the Jack Valentis and Lloyd and Ann Hand [another D.C. power couple]. They are staying in the Wasserman house. Talked to Henry Kissinger and gave him my undivided opinion about the president meeting tomorrow with the motion picture industry leaders. Jack Warner, Charles Bluhdorn, Jim Aubrey, Leo Jaffe, Taft Schreiber and Jack Valenti—that's the cast.

He wants now my list. I said to him that I will help him to solve his problems in Israel and you will help him with the film industry. He said he was willing. Anyhow, he will

take his vacation end of April until around May 6 in Palm
Springs. He refuses our house out of friendship, but hopes we
will be there at the same time.

By the way we have right now still severe aftershocks of the
big earthquake with great damage in the same area. I am stiff
with fright when the house shakes and we all meet in the hall
and run down the steps to look for more damage. So far so
good. Everybody says it is the extreme heat that does it.

I loved your letter from Oban. I love your letters. I love
you. Good night, sweet Prince. Meet me in dreamland!

Stolz

KIRK:

Henry was able to let his hair down in Hollywood. He loved to decompress with his show business friends. Returning from a trip to China, he called us from LAX. He was headed to San Clemente to give his report to President Nixon. "I thought I'd stop at your house for a quick visit before getting on the road," he said.

ANNE:

I took the phone from Kirk. "Some friends are due here for dinner," I told Henry. "It's too bad you can't stay."

I mentioned some of the guests' names, including Frank Sinatra, so I wasn't surprised when he asked if I could set another place at the table. Of course, everyone was thrilled to be hearing firsthand about Henry's follow-up trip to China after President Nixon's historic visit to that communist nation.

Time passed quickly, and it was nearly midnight—way beyond Kirk's tolerance point. I was mortified when he looked at his watch, got up, and started flicking the light switches. That put a quick end to the evening. Frank and Henry left together.

KIRK:

We were fast asleep when the phone rang around 5:00 a.m. It was the Beverly Hills chief of police, calling on behalf of President Nixon. "The president's looking for Henry Kissinger, who told him he was having dinner with you. Do you know where he is?"

I heard Anne say, "He's not here. I'll try to get a message to him." Frank Sinatra was a nocturnal animal who had probably just gotten to sleep, but Anne called him anyway.

ANNE:

I knew Kirk wouldn't make the call. Everyone walked on eggshells around Frank, never knowing if he would banish you if he didn't like what you said or did. He greeted me with, "Who the hell is calling at this hour?"

"It's Anne Douglas, Frank."

"Ah, Frenchie, what's wrong?"

"Do you know where Henry is?"

"Yeah, right here. We've been talking all night."

"Well, tell him the president is looking for him." I hung up and went back to sleep.

KIRK:

Frank never seemed to get annoyed with Anne. I was amazed. He couldn't intimidate me, but I always let him set the tone of our meetings. And we rarely had deep personal conversations. I wrote in my book, *Climbing the Mountain*, "You could be Frank's closest friend and then suddenly, for some unexplained reason, you were out. Our place in Palm Springs was often a halfway house for the people he discarded in this way. Yul Brynner had been very close to Frank, and suddenly he was out. . . . He spent a couple of weekends at our house before he was reinstated. . . . Greg and Veronique Peck spent several weekends at our halfway house before they once again became part of Frank's in-crowd. Pat DiCicco was pathetic during his expulsion. Leo Durocher, manager of the Dodgers, was devastated when he lost favor."

Frank never banished the Douglases, and we've been equally fortunate in our other friendships, due mainly to Anne's popularity.

We lost Nelson Rockefeller in 1979, and I sent Henry a mournful letter from London, where I was making a science-fiction thriller called *Saturn 3*. Here's Henry's reply:

> **Dear Kirk:**
>
> *Your very thoughtful letter was here on our return from Acapulco. I remember so many happy occasions with the Douglases, the Bradens and Nelson that it is still hard to believe he is gone.*
>
> *I can't say I have much sympathy for you, however, all by yourself in London with Farrah Fawcett-Majors. Grandfather or not, it's not a bad way to earn a living!*
>
> *I agree that it has been much too long since we've seen you. Why not stop in New York or Washington on your way home?*
>
>

> **Warm regards,**
> **Henry**
>

ANNE:

We continued to be invited to the White House for state dinners and for special occasions such as the Kennedy Center Honors. I asked Kirk to write the letters after such events. His note to Pat Nixon is undated, but it was obviously before August 9, 1974, when the president resigned, and Gerald Ford selected our friend Nelson as his Veep. (We got to know the Fords very well when they moved to the desert.)

> **Dear Mrs. Nixon:**
>
> *I must tell you again how thrilled and delighted my wife and I were to be invited to the White House dinner for Prime Minister Heath. It was a fascinating and charming evening.*
>
> *I risked not being invited back again, because I'm the one that moved the container of flowers on the table that was*

*obstructing my view of your daughter, Julie—a sight more
beautiful than a bouquet of flowers.*

Many thanks and a wonderful New Year to you, the president, and your family.

Sincerely,
Kirk

KIRK:

I was getting older, and life was throwing us a few curves. We lost good friends; we were dealing with Eric's bipolar condition and drug dependence; I was getting used to fans coming up and saying, "Wow, Michael Douglas's father!"

Anne was working harder than ever. I had asked her to be president of the Bryna Company because we worked so well together. I only wanted to be concerned with artistic matters, and she had a natural talent for business and contracts. She took over when Peter and Eric were too busy with their own activities to care if she was home with them. She had even taken over as producer of *Scalawag*, my first directing effort, which we shot in Italy and Yugoslavia. Our enterprising seventeen-year-old Peter was the still photographer. He got Lesley-Anne Down, also seventeen, to sign a contract allowing him to do a nude layout, which he promptly sold to *Playboy*. Peter was the only Douglas to make a profit on that film.

Thank God for our diplomatic and political friends. The times we spent with them, away from the movie business, were wonderful respites from our problems. We became close to Jimmy and Rosalynn Carter, a bond that endures to this day. On December 18, 1979, I received this from President Carter on White House stationery:

To Kirk Douglas
*The seventh day of Christmas will be particularly memorable
for us because of your singing during the State Dinner for
Prime Minister Thatcher last night.*

The caroling was enjoyable and Rosalynn and I appreciate your generous spirit!

Sincerely,
Jimmy Carter

Fiftieth wedding anniversary, Kirk marries "a nice Jewish girl"

ANNE:

Although neither Kirk nor I were Reagan supporters during his successful runs for governor of California and president of the United States, we were still friends. As a breast cancer survivor, Nancy was able to lean on me for advice and comfort during her own diagnosis and treatment. We spent happy hours with Nancy and Ron at White House functions, Music Center events, and Sunnylands parties.

During the president's long decline into Alzheimer's and after his demise, Nancy and I met regularly for lunch. Every few weeks Kirk and I would have laughter-filled, gossipy dinners with Nancy and Merv Griffin. She and Merv were at our second wedding celebration, on the occasion of our fiftieth anniversary, May 29, 2004—a happy occasion eclipsed less than two months later when our son Eric died of an overdose.

Nancy had weathered problems with her rebellious daughter Patti during the White House days, but her most personal trauma was the attempt on her beloved Ronnie's life. Kirk was filming *The Man from Snowy River* in Australia when the president was shot. He immediately wrote a heartfelt letter, to which Nancy replied, in her distinctive handwriting.

> *Dear Kirk—*
> *Thank you for your nice letter and for all the information on your Australian stay and their reaction to the assassination attempt. I must admit I still can't believe it really happened—*

it's like a nightmare—one that's over, thank God, but still lingers on—I'm beginning to think it always will. But it was a miracle—God was really looking out for us—

I read about Peter and am so glad he seems to be doing so well.

Thanks again for your thoughtfulness in writing—My very best to you and Anne—

Nancy

KIRK:

When William Jefferson Clinton took office, I realized that all presidents from now on would be more of Michael's generation than mine. I felt passionate about his pledge to lift the ban on gays in the military. It was yet another example of hypocrisy like the blacklist. President Clinton was kind enough to write me a handwritten note in his left-handed slant:

Dear Kirk

Thank you for your letter on gays in the military—I hope you will speak out—we need help to prevail and we should.

Sincerely,
Bill Clinton

I also wrote to Hillary Clinton about her efforts to reform health care. She wrote back with the kind of detailed consideration we have come to expect of her. As I write this in November 2016, I have just placed my absentee ballot in the mail; I voted for Hillary. It will undoubtedly be the last vote of my life. I shake my head in wonder. I was born in 1916, four years before the ratification of the Nineteenth Amendment by an all-male Congress finally allowed women to vote.

FROM TOP: *Three of Anita May's protégées, left to right: Harriet Deutsch, Anne, and Nancy Reagan at the Annenbergs for New Year's Eve • President Clinton and Kirk at the Beverly Hilton Hotel*

August 18, 1993

Dear Kirk:

As a longtime fan of your work, I was delighted to receive your letter. The president joins me in offering our thanks to you for your many years of quality movie making and for your obvious deep concern for the future of our country.

I appreciate your suggestions regarding reforming our national health care system. The challenge of changing this huge, bureaucratic system is as formidable as you suggest, but as I traveled the country, I have found that Americans are willing, even eager to support a new plan that is balanced and fair. You are right on target in pointing out that individuals and private groups must assume more responsibility. Your views were helpful as we finalize plans for the Administration's initiative.

Thank you for writing. I appreciate your invitation to visit the Motion Picture and Television Country Home and Hospital. It sounds as though you are doing tremendous work.

Sincerely yours,
Hillary

ANNE:

I am so proud of the way my husband has used his celebrity to support worthy causes and speak out for his beliefs. He is also quick to write congratulatory letters which, because of his fame, are usually answered just as quickly. Here's one to and from President Obama after his historic election in 2008:

November 7, 2008

Dear Mr. President,
This is a happy day for my wife, me, and my staff.
 This is what I heard on Public Radio:
 Rosa sat so Martin could walk.
 Martin walked so Barack could run.
 Barack ran so our children could fly.
 May God look after you and your family.

Sincerely,
Kirk Douglas

November 20, 2008

Dear Kirk,
I just wanted to send this note to thank you for your kind words. Your films have inspired generations of Americans, and I appreciated your heartwarming message.

I've traveled to every corner of the country over the past 21 months. I've heard countless stories that I will take with me to the White House, stories of hope, promise, and opportunity. They are part of the larger American story we will continue to write in the years to come. There is no question that our work is only beginning. Our nation faces enormous tasks ahead, but if the American people stay engaged, I have no doubt that we will rise to the main challenges of our time.

Once again, Kirk, thanks so much for your letter, and please give my regards to your family. I'm so pleased that we are moving into a brighter future together.

Sincerely,
Barack Obama

Eight years later, President Obama also sent Kirk a letter on the occasion of his 100th birthday:

> **Kirk—**
>
> *As a big fan of your work, and an admirer of your work on behalf of so many social causes over the years, let me wish you a joyous 100th birthday.*
>
> *What an amazing contribution you've made to America. We are grateful!*
>
> **Barack Obama**

THE WHITE HOUSE

WASHINGTON

Kirk —

As a big fan of your work, and an admirer of your work on behalf of so many social causes over the years, let me wish you a joyous 100th birthday.

What an amazing contribution you've made to America. We are grateful!

CHAPTER TWELVE

Friends and Family

KIRK:

I don't go to my Bryna Company offices anymore. It no longer gives me pleasure to look at the signed posters of my movies hanging there. I've outlived many of the friends I worked with and I miss them. I also miss the camaraderie we shared in locations all over the world.

Ninety movies in sixty years—impressive, right? Seven films with Burt; three each with John Wayne, Tony Curtis, Vincente Minnelli; two with Tony Quinn, Lauren Bacall, Walter Matthau, Yul Brynner; only one with Frank Sinatra and my favorite costar of all, Michael Douglas.

When I think of it, we were primarily a bunch of left-leaning liberals. All except for John Wayne, a conservative Republican through and through. He approved of the blacklist and supported candidates like Barry Goldwater. We pretended to be more bothered by our differences than we were, and we were very fond of each other.

In 1966, John and I were in Durango, Mexico, shooting *The War Wagon* for his independent company, Batjac. A few weeks before election day, we were photographed casting our absentee ballots for the California gubernatorial race. John, of course, was voting for Ronald Reagan and I was supporting Governor Pat Brown.

AP's side by side captioned photos ran everywhere. Governor Brown enclosed the clipping in this letter he sent me:

October 27, 1966

Dear Kirk:

Thank you for your kind letter. I am enclosing pictures appearing in the Sacramento Union *today of both you and John Wayne completing your absentee ballots. I must say that Mr. Wayne looks far less confident of his decision than you do.*

Perhaps he is really one of those undecided voters who will be so crucial on November 8.

Kirk, your TV spot has been marvelously received, although there are a few of my back-sliding friends who are claiming that perhaps you would have made a better candidate than I.

With best wishes and many thanks for all your help,

Sincerely,

Pat

EDMUND G. BROWN, Governor

ANNE:

I went to Durango, even though Kirk warned me of the primitive accommodations at the Super-Motel where the company was based. I was feeling adventurous and lonely for my husband, so I decided it was worth a little discomfort.

Sitting at the entrance of cabana 3 of the motel when I arrived was Robert Walker Jr., the son of our friend Jennifer Jones and her ex-husband Robert Walker. Bobby wasn't on call that day so Kirk asked him to look after me. We went into what passed for a suite, and I said I'd meet Bobby after I cleaned up. I went to the bathroom and was hit by a sign pasted on the mirror. I thought it was probably a reminder to use only bottled water for brushing one's teeth. But here was a health notice I'd never seen anywhere: "Shake out your boots and check for tarantulas and scorpions before putting them on." That did it. I marched to the Production Office and told them to book me on the next plane home.

California voters John Wayne, left, and Kirk Douglas cast absentee ballots in the middle of an Indian war of sorts in Durango, Mexico. Wayne is a strong supporter of Ronald Reagan and Douglas is an equally strong backer of Governor Brown. — (AP Photos)

EDMUND G. BROWN

GOVERNOR

SACRAMENTO, CALIFORNIA

October 27, 1966

Mr. Kirk Douglas
Campo Mexico Courts, S.A.
Super-Motel
Ave. 20 de Nov. Ext. Ote.
APDO. 96
Durango, Dgo., Mexico

Dear Kirk:

Thank you for your kind letter. I am enclosing pictures appearing in the Sacramento Union today of both you and John Wayne completing your absentee ballots. I must say that Mr. Wayne looks far less confident of his decision tha
Perhaps he is really

When Kirk arrived, I greeted him with my packed bag already in the car. "You were right, darling," I said, "so hello and good-bye."

Duke's Peruvian wife, Pilar, had more guts than I did; she stuck around. Here's a letter Kirk wrote her several months after the film wrapped:

> **Dear Pilar:**
>
> *Wherein did I fail? It's now almost two months since the finish of* War Wagon, *and Duke hasn't come to me with another script. What did I do wrong?*
>
> *After all, when he needed someone to help him hold up the War Wagon, who did he come to? Precious!*
>
> *When he got in that stupid brawl in the barroom, who kicked the gun out of the hand that was going to shoot him? Precious!*
>
> *When he needed someone to open up the safe and get the nitroglycerin for that drunken buddy of his, who did it? That's right. Precious!*
>
> *That's what he thinks, because I found out where he kept it and used some of it to make this flower for you. Don't you think it's precious?*
>
> **Affectionately,**
> **Kirk**

KIRK:

A year before *The War Wagon*, I was in another film with Wayne. *Cast a Giant Shadow* was about Colonel Mickey Marcus, an American hero of Israel's War of Independence. A graduate of West Point, Mickey had been highly decorated for his service in World War II. After the Jewish State was declared in 1947, war with the surrounding Arab nations was inevitable. The retired Army colonel was recruited to train the neophyte Israeli troops. They won the war, but Mickey was killed by friendly fire from a nervous Israeli sentry.

John Wayne sent me the script. He said, "It's a great part for you. I'm going to play an American general, and Yul Brynner and Frank Sinatra have agreed to be in it."

How could I say no to that? If nothing else, the four of us would have fun. I came with my son the driver (Michael) and my son the bodyguard (Joel). I thought they would have fun, too. *Cast a Giant Shadow* was Mel Shavelson's passion project. He couldn't get funding until he got Duke interested. Wayne liked the idea of an American military hero coming to the aid of a weak young democracy. Wayne's Batjac Productions and my Bryna Company joined Llenroc Productions and the Mirisch Corporation in the financing.

Oy veh! It was 126 degrees in the desert, but *tsuros* with the military was even more scorching. Yitzhak Rabin—later to become prime minister and my good friend—was commander-in-chief of the Israeli armed forces; he demanded script approval. There was also a military committee to review the footage. They insisted Mel reshoot a scene of young people dancing the hora because one of the girls was out of step.

One day, a hundred Israeli tanks took off in the middle of the movie's battle scene to go to a real one on the Syrian border. On another—in what reminded me of my Norwegian *Vikings* experience—two hundred Israeli extras walked out halfway through the day. They returned hours later and announced they had formed the Israeli Screen Extras Guild and wanted triple pay.

ANNE:

I heard the guys were raising holy hell in the Holy Land, so I packed up Peter and Eric and went off to see for myself how badly they had corrupted Michael and Joel. I hoped they were staying away from the *sabra* women—a tough bunch of beauties who were handy with guns.

One night around midnight, while Frank, Yul, Duke, and Kirk were filming a street scene, Frank said, "Sure would like a plate of pasta."

There was something about Sinatra that made you want to please him. But to find an Italian restaurant in Jerusalem and one open past midnight was akin to an Old Testament miracle. In this case Yul Brynner was the miracle worker. "Boys," he said triumphantly, "come with me. It's all arranged. We're having pasta at the best Chinese restaurant in Israel. Don't forget, it was Chinese before Marco Polo brought it to Italy."

Yul, a true citizen of the world, seemed to know everything and everybody. Yet, he maintained a certain air of mysterious glamour even with those of us who were close friends.

KIRK:

John Wayne was larger than life, a gentle soul who loved to play chess and would only ride a horse when he was paid to do so. I never called him Duke. I don't know how or when he acquired the nickname, but I bet he dumped his given name of Marion Morrison because it didn't suit his macho image. He felt that stars like us should play tough both on and off the screen.

Years later, it was hard to see John, the American hero in so many war films, battling cancer. He had won his first fight against the disease in his lungs, but then it moved to his stomach. While he was at Massachusetts General Hospital in Boston for treatment, I sent him two mailgrams on April 21, 1978—the year before he died. The hospital's address was 32 Fruit Street:

> **DEAR JOHN,**
> **I DIDN'T WANT TO WRITE YOU ON FRUIT STREET. I HAVE**
> **BEEN WAITING FOR YOU TO MOVE TO MACHO ALLEY.**
> **WHAT THE HELL . . . GET WELL SOON**
> **KIRK DOUGLAS**

A few hours later I followed it up with this:

> **DEAR JOHN,**
> **DURING THE PASSOVER HOLIDAYS I WILL PRAY TO MY**
> **GOD JEHOVAH FOR YOUR QUICK RECOVERY AND TO**
> **INSURE A RESPONSE I WILL NOT MENTION THAT IT WAS**
> **A NON-KOSHER OPERATION.**
> **KIRK DOUGLAS**

On April 26, he replied:

> **DEAR KIRK,**
> **THANKS FOR THE TELEGRAMS. OH BY THE WAY WHILE**
> **I WAS HERE I HAD A LITTLE SORT OF DIMPLE PUT IN MY**
> **CHIN. I KNEW YOU WOULDN'T MIND**
> **DUKE**

ANNE:

Kirk was realistic enough to accept that things were changing for actors, especially for ones getting on in years. It was no longer anathema to take a good role on television. Karl Malden, after all, seemed happy enough working with Michael in *The Streets of San Francisco*. Tony Curtis was in England doing a series with Roger Moore called *The Persuaders*. Kirk, too, took on more work for the small screen.

In 1982, he did *Remembrance of Love* in Israel and we were very proud of our son Eric's performance in that film. Our son Peter won an Emmy for producing the 1988 TV version of *Inherit the Wind*. Peter also produced the theatrical feature *The Final Countdown* under his Vincent Pictures banner. We were impressed that he got the navy's permission to shoot on the U.S.S. *Nimitz*.

All four of the young men in our family chose to work in "The Industry" either in front of or behind the camera. Joel ran Victorine Studios in Nice, France, before returning to the States to produce films with Michael. Like any Jewish father, Kirk had hoped at least one would be a doctor or lawyer.

KIRK:

Michael was hosting the 1985 Academy Awards, and Burt and I agreed to be presenters. What a thrill it was for me to have Michael introduce us with a clip from our 1958 appearance doing *It's Great Not to Be Nominated*. We were a hit with two young writers in the audience. They looked at each other and said, "Let's write a film for them." Disney liked the idea and so did we. We were working on *Tough Guys* later that year.

TONY CURTIS

June 5
19 64

Dear Kirk:

How did you know I love to look at my face?

It's by far the best thing I've seen!
Those cruelly, penetrating blue eyes - - the
dark, impertinent hair - the very expressive
eyebrows - those mobile and sensuous lips -
that fabulously cut jaw---------------oh shit,
I'm in love again!!

Thank you.

Affectionately,

TC
jw

Relaxing in Palm Springs, left to right: Tony Curtis, Kirk, and Dean Martin

Burt and I loved the story of two old geezers who get out of jail after sharing a tiny cell for thirty years. They decide to take another crack at the botched robbery that landed them behind bars. In one scene I got to slam dance, in another I ran on top of a moving train and mooned Charles Durning. The hardest thing about that stunt was convincing Anne I wasn't too old to do it. After all, I still had a few months to go before turning seventy.

Ever since a fan called out to me "Hey, Koik! How's Boit?" at a Dodgers game in Brooklyn, that's what we called each other. But when I sent Burt this birthday telegram on November 1, 1985, we were still in our *Tough Guys* mindset as our characters, Harry (Burt) and Archie (me):

> **DEAR HARRY: I HAVE BEEN LIVING IN A NURSING HOME FOR SOMETIME. THE GUY NEXT TO ME GOT KNOCKED OFF. THE BED IS EMPTY. IT IS YOURS IF YOU WANT IT. HAPPY BIRTHDAY.**
> **LOVE ARCHIE**

Here is Burt's reply of November 7:

> **DEAR ARCHIE**
> **NOW WHAT WOULD I WANT WITH AN EMPTY BED? BUT THANKS FOR THE THOUGHT**
> **LOVE AND KISSES**
> **HARRY**

ANNE:

I fell in love with Kirk the night he swept up the elephant poop at the *Cirque d'Hiver*. We both are irritated by pompous people who can't laugh at themselves. No such problem with Tony Curtis. Here's a thank you note from him dated June 5, 1964, that made it into my collection of memorabilia. I suspect the gift was a photo in a fancy frame:

Dear Kirk:

How did you know I love to look at my face?

It's by far the best thing I've seen!

Those cruelly, penetrating blue eyes—the dark, impertinent hair—the very expressive eyebrows—those mobile and sensuous lips—that fabulously cut jaw——————oh shit,

I'm in love again!!

Thank you.

Affectionately,
Tony

KIRK:

When I was in town, I liked to lunch at the Hillcrest Country Club (where the food was great) or at the Friars Club in Beverly Hills (where the food was not), but only if I could snag a spot at the comedians' table. It was a chance to *kibbutz* with Jack Benny, George Burns, Georgie Jessel, Milton Berle, Red Buttons, Don Rickles, Groucho Marx, or whoever else turned up.

I adored those guys and their Yiddish-tinged humor. Even their written notes were clever, like this undated one from Red Buttons:

Dear Kirk,

To answer your question "How did you manage to get such a beautiful wife?"

It's all in the wrist!

A hug for you and Anne

With love
Red

———————— | ★ | ————————

ANNE:

As you might imagine for a man who has been on the so-called A-list for some seventy years, Kirk has received multiple tributes in America and abroad. In addition to the Medal of Freedom, he received the Medal of the Arts from President George W. Bush, the Legion d'Honneur from the French government, a Kennedy Center Honor, the AFI Lifetime Achievement, and an Honorary Oscar. These last two were particularly meaningful because of the dramatic life-threatening events that preceded them: a back-breaking helicopter crash and the stroke that left him with impaired speech.

KIRK:

I was always more comfortable being a presenter than an honoree. My friend "Boit," who emceed my tribute from the American Academy of Dramatic Arts, knew I never ate before making a speech. After I delivered my words, I sat down and looked at him expectantly: "How was I?" I asked. "Koik," he replied, "You could have eaten."

The shortest speech I ever gave was the one at the 1996 Oscars. Unable to utter coherent words when the letter about my Honorary Oscar arrived, I asked Michael to accept on my behalf. I wasn't ready or able to face the public yet. "Work with your speech therapist, Dad, because I am going to watch you from the audience."

I learned to say two words, "thank you," pretty clearly. I could handle two syllables. But I wasn't satisfied. It was just the incentive I needed to surprise my family and the worldwide audience with something more. From the stage I pointed to my four sons sitting in the audience: "They are proud of the Old Man," I said clearly. I held up the Oscar: "Anne, this is for you." I could see her crying in the audience, ruining the beautiful makeup job she had left the house with. I got a standing ovation.

What an outpouring of letters from everywhere. Gena Rowlands, my wonderful costar in *Lonely Are the Brave*, Bruce and Patti Springsteen, Goldie Hawn, Janet Leigh, Patricia Neal (who had come back from a more severe stroke than mine to act again), and even King Hussein of Jordan, who invited me to be his guest in Amman when I felt well enough.

Robin Williams wrote:

Mazeltov!
Remember the mohel* gets final cut.

Robin Williams

*mohel: Hebrew name for one who performs ritual circumcisions

Jerry Seinfeld, another comic genius, said simply:

Dear Kirk
Congratulations on achieving legend status as an artist and as a man. No one more than me is grateful for you having blazed the trail in our business for good looking on camera Jews.

Mazel tov,
Jerry Seinfeld

Billy Crystal—one of my favorite Oscar hosts—wrote in a more serious vein in a letter dated March 28, 1996:

Dear Kirk
Watching your brave appearance on the "Oscars" is one I will never forget. One can only hope that their families will look at them with the same love that your lovely wife and sons looked at you with. You are Spartacus!
With my best wishes and thank you for all the inspiration—get well soon.

Billy Crystal

ROBIN

To Kirk

mazeltov!

Remember the mohel ge[...]
final cut.

R. William
WILLIAMS

Dear Kirk

Congratulations on
achieving legend
status as an artist
and as a man.
No one more than
me is grateful
for you having blazed
the trail ~~x~~ in
our business for
good looking
on camera Jews

Mazel Tov,

Jerry Seinfeld

Steven Spielberg, whom I admire and love, had introduced me in such laudatory terms I wanted to cry. Here is an earlier exchange between us:

February 7, 1994

Dear Steven,

You deserve all of the success you have had with your films. It gave you the power--you always had the talent--to make "Schindler's List". What a movie! A historical piece of film.

I am now in the process of writing my fifth book--not a novel. Here I try to grapple with what it means to be a Jew. You, much younger than I, have wrestled successfully.

I only have four sons. I think I'll adopt you, too.

With much affection,

קירק

KD/lm

FEB 1 6 1994

11 February 1994

Kirk Douglas
805 North Rexford Drive
Beverly Hills, California 90210

Dear Kirk,

I thought those twelve nominations gave me a boost through the roof, but your letter pushed me all the way up into the plumbing!

By the way, consider me adopted. i love making you proud.

Your friend,

Dear Steven,

You deserve all the success you have had with your films. It gave you the power—you always had the talent—to make Schindler's List. *What a movie! A historical piece of film.*

I am now in the progress of writing my fifth book not a novel. Here I try to grapple with what it means to be a Jew. You, much younger than I, have wrestled successfully.

I only have four sons. I think I'll adopt you, too.

With much affection,
Kirk

Dear Kirk,

I thought those twelve nominations game me a boost through the roof, but your letter pushed me all the way up into the plumbing!

By the way, consider me adopted. I love making you proud.

Your friend,
Steven

It was hard to believe that only a few months before receiving my honorary Oscar, I had been in the depths of despair, feeling so sorry for myself I pulled out the gun I had saved from *Gunfight at the O.K. Corral* to kill myself. I kept thinking: What does an actor do who can't talk? Wait for silent pictures to come back?

Instead, I took stock of what else life had in store for me. I had been lucky—even with my stroke. Burt had lost both speech and movement after his stroke. I was no longer young, and I didn't know how long God's reprieve would last, but I was ready for my next act, as long as I could share it with Anne.

CHAPTER THIRTEEN

Caring Is Sharing

KIRK:

I have great admiration for the way Christopher Reeve, Michael J. Fox (my costar in *Greedy*), and so many others in my profession have used their physical challenges to raise awareness and monies for research. Sometimes, we actors can even make a difference when our performances shed light on a problem, like my role as a victim of elder abuse in the television drama, *Amos.*

After I went onstage before millions of viewers all over the world at the Oscars, I became the "poster boy" for stroke victims. I received a great many letters from people who were struggling or had a friend or family member who was in despair.

I had been more fortunate than many who have similar brain attacks. I didn't die, and only my speech was severely affected. I would still be able to play golf, and I could learn to speak again if I was diligent about my exercises. But in those early days, I couldn't talk and I couldn't stop drooling. One side of my mouth sagged, and I was a sorry sight. Thank God for Anne's tough love, or I would have wallowed forever in self-pity.

I spoke at conventions of speech therapists; I raised money for stroke awareness; most important, I tried to answer the letters of everyone who wrote me to urge them not to give up. Eventually, I wrote a book called *My Stroke of Luck*, in which I described my suicidal depression and what I did to get over it. I included my personal six-point prescription, which

I called an Operator's Manual:

1. When things go bad, always remember it could be worse.
2. Never, never give up. Keep working on your speech and on your life.
3. Never lose your sense of humor. Laugh at yourself. Laugh with others.
4. Stem depression by thinking of, reaching out to, and helping others. Strive to be a Little Hero.
5. Do unto others as you would have them do unto you.
6. Pray. Not for God to cure you, but to help you help yourself.

ANNE:

Kirk was shocked—I wasn't—at how people responded to his honesty and courage. After all, in America alone, approximately 700,000 people a year have strokes, and many of them are young. He was well aware that his celebrity status helped make his voice (impaired as it was) an important instrument of hope.

One of the most poignant letters he received was from the brilliant actress Julie Harris, printed with obvious difficulty on August 2, 2001, three months after her first stroke.

> **Dear Kirk,**
> *I am thinking of you and hope you are doing well.*
>
> *In May I suffered a slight stroke, which has left me with difficulty in speaking. I am now home in Chatham, MA, taking intensive speech therapy.*
>
> *I am inspired by your recovery. I think youre [sic] a wonderful person, and a superb actor and writer.*
>
> *I love you,*
> *Julie Harris*

SIMPLE AND ACTOR and
writer.

I love you,
Julie Harris

Aug. 2, 01

AUG 07 2001

Dear Kirk,
I am thinking of you and
hope you are doing well.
An May I Suffered a
slight Stroke, which has
left me with difficulty
is speaking. I am Now
home in Chatham, MA at
MA, taking intensive
Speesh Therapy.
I Am inspired by
your Recovery. and
your
I think youre A Wonderful
Person, AND A Superb

KIRK DOUGLAS

August 8, 2001

Julie Harris
132 Barnhill Road
West Chatham, MA 02669

Dear Julie,

I was happy to hear from you, and very happy that you're
working with your speech therapist. Don't give up!
Sometimes, you will feel like you're not making progress.
That's the time to work harder. It won't be long before we
talk together. My book, My Stroke of Luck, will be coming out
at the end of the year. I will send you a copy. You might find
it helpful.

There is a reason for everything in life, and you will find the
reason.

Love,

Kirk Douglas

SEPTEMBER 24, 2002

Stonewall, Texas

DEAR ANNE AND KIRK,

    <u>MY STROKE OF LUCK</u> CONTAINS SO MANY ELEMENTS. IT IS A CELEBRATION OF LIFE AND LOVE, AN OVERCOMING OF FEAR AND FRAILTIES, AN INSIGHT INTO THE HUMAN CONDITION AND A GIFT OF HOPE.

    IT BUOYED ME TO HAVE IT READ TO ME. NEARLY FIVE MONTHS AFTER MY STROKE, I AM STILL STRUGGLING TO SPEAK WELL ENOUGH TO BE UNDERSTOOD. I INCH ALONG WITH TWICE DAILY SESSIONS WITH MY SPEECH THERAPIST (NOT TO MENTION A TEAM OF OTHER THERAPISTS), AND I'M TOLD I'M MAKING PROGRESS. BUT WITH FAMILY WATCHING OVER ME, I'M 'OUT AND ABOUT' GOING TO DINNER AND THE RANCH ON WEEKENDS. AND AFTER ALL THESE YEARS, I FINALLY HAVE A PLAUSIBLE EXCUSE TO SAY NO TO THINGS I DON'T WANT TO DO!

    KIRK, I THINK WHAT YOU'VE WRITTEN SO MASTERFULLY WILL BE A BOON NOT ONLY TO STROKE VICTIMS AND THEIR FAMILIES, BUT CAREGIVERS AS WELL. I SALUTE YOU FROM THE BOTTOM OF MY HEART.

    SO FONDLY,

Lady Bird Johnson

Kirk's immediate reply (the day after the letter came) was typical of his caring:

> **Dear Julie,**
>
> *I was happy to hear from you, and very happy that you're working with your speech therapist. Don't give up! Sometimes, you will feel like you're not making progress. That's the time to work harder. It won't be long before we talk together. My book,* My Stroke of Luck, *will be coming out at the end of the year. I will send you a copy. You might find it helpful.*
>
>   *There is a reason for everything in life, and you will find the reason.*
>
>   **Love,**
>   **Kirk Douglas**

Lady Bird Johnson, our dear friend of so many years, also had a severe stroke. Her daughter, Luci, read her *My Stroke of Luck*, because, in addition to her impairments from the stroke, she had severe macular degeneration. I treasure the letter she sent on September 24, 2002:

> **Dear Anne and Kirk,**
>
> My Stroke of Luck *contains so many elements. It is a celebration of life and love, an overcoming of fear and frailties, an insight into the human condition, and a gift of hope.*
>
>   *It buoyed me to have it read to me. Nearly five months after my stroke, I am still struggling to speak well enough to be understood. I inch along with twice daily sessions with my speech therapist (not to mention a team of other therapists), and I'm told I am making progress. But with family watching over me, I'm "out and about" going to dinner and the ranch on weekends. And after all these years, I finally have a plausible excuse to say no to things I don't want to do.*

Kirk, I think what you've written so masterfully will be a boon not only to stroke victims and their families, but caregivers as well. I salute you from the bottom of my heart.

So fondly,
Lady Bird Johnson

KIRK:

People in show business are often depicted as egotistical and hedonistic. No doubt, some elements of those characteristics creep in, especially for the few of us who—deservedly or not—are idolized by the public, not necessarily for our achievements but simply because we're famous.

For some in our community, fame is the drug. For others, like Robert Downey Jr., the drug is a sickness called addiction. Because of our son Eric, we know too well the heartbreak of those who struggle and lose. So, I'm glad that Robert has achieved such soaring personal and professional success.

I was very worried about him when he was sentenced to serve time in a California correctional facility. I didn't really know him, but I was familiar with the kind of demons that tormented him. I wanted him to know I cared. This is what I wrote on December 13, 1999:

Dear Robert,

Please forgive my Chutzpah in writing this letter. I admire you as an actor. You have great talent. A talent such as yours is given to you by God. You have the responsibility of preserving that talent.

You cannot use that talent where you are now. It may sound pretentious, but I believe sincerely that when you have such a talent, you have an obligation to other people.

I pray that God will give you the strength to deal with your problems so that we may enjoy your talent in the future.

Sincerely,
Kirk Douglas

P.S. I must admit that I have one son that I have not been very successful with my advice. But maybe I will be more successful with you.

He sent back a postcard in bright red ink. It was Christmas Eve:

KD,
I'm no schmuck.
When advice comes from a good man, I take it!
Hey! What a privilege to be in your thoughts.

—Downey

KIRK DOUGLAS

December 13, 1999

Mr. Robert Downey, Jr.
P50522-F1a117LCSATS
California Substance Abuse Facility, S.P.
P.O. Box 5244
Corcoran, CA 93212

Dear Robert,

Please forgive my Chutzpah in writing this letter. I admire you as an actor. You have great talent. A talent such as yours is given to you by God. You have the responsibility of preserving that talent.

You cannot use that talent where you are now. It may sound pretentious, but I believe sincerely that when you have such a talent, you have an obligation to other people.

I pray that God will give you the strength to deal with your problems so that we may enjoy your talent in the future.

Sincerely,

Kirk Douglas

P.S. I must admit that I have one son that I have not been very successful with my advice. But maybe I will be more successful with you.

ANNE:

I believe that words and personal involvement are wonderful, but money is even better. We formed the Douglas Foundation in 1964, after films like *Spartacus* and *Seven Days in May* replenished our finances.

Lew Wasserman advised me that when it comes to philanthropy, it is better to find a few causes you can fund generously rather than diluting your impact with small donations to everything. That advice resonated with me, but we couldn't really implement it on the scale I envisioned without making a few sacrifices.

KIRK:

Anne is referring, of course, to the sale of major pieces from our art collection at Christie's in May of 1990. We had been collecting seriously since our marriage in 1954, and the collection had appreciated substantially in the art boom of the century's final two decades. The only art piece I owned when we married was a large poster by Toulouse-Lautrec of Aristide Bruant, the Parisian nightclub entertainer. He is wearing a black cape with a crimson scarf and a large black hat worn at a rakish angle. The lithograph cost $500, a fortune at the time, and I framed it myself with the help of a friend. We kept that piece out of the sale, as well as a few lovely paintings Anne brought with her from Paris.

In all, we sent fifty-two pieces to the auction, which was held in New York over several days—the most valuable paintings and sculpture on the first, the lesser pieces later on.

When Christie's came to remove the art, Anne started crying uncontrollably. Each piece was a memory: Chagall's *Night Rider* from the artist's Mexican period and a Vlaminck painting of flowers were two pieces she and Fran Stark had borrowed for the party I gave her in 1954. There were other Chagalls we acquired from the master himself and works by Braque, Miró, Vuillard, Balthus, and even an early portrait by the great modernist Piet Mondrian.

I was no help. I took off for the golf course to play eighteen holes to avoid the disturbing scene.

ANNE:

The sale was Kirk's idea, and I had resisted it at first. He explained that we wouldn't give up collecting. We would just acquire emerging contemporary artists who were destined to be great. Meanwhile, we would use most of the proceeds from the sale to finance the big dreams I was starting to have for the foundation.

Kirk told a reporter from the *Los Angeles Times*: "When you reach a certain standard of living you should help those who are less fortunate."

KIRK:

I learned that lesson from my mother, Bryna. When I was a child, I was puzzled that she would never turn away the hobos who came to our door. She always found a little morsel of food for them. I didn't understand. I knew how little we had, and how often my stomach would growl in protest. Ma patiently explained: "Even a beggar must give to a person who has less." She maintained a little blue box, a *puschka*, into which she dropped a few coins for charity whenever she could.

ANNE:

One of the first things I wanted to do with the enhanced funds of the Douglas Foundation was help the homeless women on skid row. We went to the Los Angeles Mission, and I started looking around the facility. There were just a few cots set up for women, with only a bedsheet to insure their privacy and safety.

I had seen so much homelessness and misery during the war, and I knew how easy it was for people to give up on themselves, especially women.

For twenty-five years, the women who go through the twelve-month rehabilitation program at the Anne Douglas Center have been part of my extended family. I am proud of their successes and I am there for them if they slip.

Kirk has his name on many buildings. This is the only one I wanted my name on. I brought my son Eric to the Anne Douglas Center on a number of occasions to speak with the women and to see what we do there. I hoped he might want to run it, but God had other plans for my troubled boy.

KIRK:

We are still a two-newspaper household. I read the *New York Times* and Anne reads the *Los Angeles Times*. She, therefore, is much better informed than I about what is happening in the Greater Los Angeles area.

One day in 1997, she came into my den with an all too familiar look of determination. "Read this," she said. "I need to do something about it."

It was a story about public schools in the huge Los Angeles School District. So many of their playgrounds were too unsafe for the kids to use. "In a country like this, in a city like Los Angeles!" she railed. "How can this be?"

By the next day, she had set up a meeting with Mayor Richard Riordan at City Hall; she brought two of her friends with charitable foundations with her. The Anne and Kirk Douglas Playground Award program was up and running with several million dollars in funding by the end of the week. That's my Anne!

Whenever I asked what I could do, she would say, "Get a job. We need the money."

Every Wednesday for eleven years, Anne would shake me awake and say, "Get ready. We'll be late for school."

We attended every dedication of every new playground. I had more fun than the kids. Actors never grow up. My big finale—after the speeches, the ribbon cutting, and the adorable performances by the kids—was going down the slide. I took my last trip with my new bionic knees when I was a mere ninety-one.

ANNE:

People don't always realize the importance of play to a child. Aside from the physical benefits in an age of childhood obesity, it is the one place where children of all backgrounds and ethnicities can socialize and learn to respect one another.

We funded several playgrounds in Israel for that very reason, praying that Arab and Jewish kids would see how alike they were on a soccer field or on a swing. We had an opportunity to visit them in 2000.

KIRK:

Kirk shows the kids how to ride a slide at a school playground dedication

Our next big investment was the Alzheimer's unit at the Motion Picture Country Home, which I named Harry's Haven for my father. He didn't have Alzheimer's but it sounded like the name of a saloon. Pa would have liked that.

I wanted to provide a place that was inviting not only to the patients, but to their loved ones. Our good friend Roddy McDowall built a garden for the families to enjoy. Now it is being enlarged into an impressive new building that will bear the name Kirk Douglas Care Pavilion.

I had been contributing to the Motion Picture Relief Fund, now the Motion Picture and Television Fund, since my early days in movies. It meets the medical and retirement needs of people in our entertainment industry, regardless of ability to pay. If Anne didn't take such good care of me, I would go live there myself! It's beautiful.

Alzheimer's is such a heartbreak. We watched as Ronnie Reagan slipped farther into the past. He didn't remember being the Leader of the Free World. But it was Nancy who bore the pain on a daily basis.

Charlton Heston announced his diagnosis in 2002. He was a lot like John Wayne politically, but I liked him although I didn't like his stance on guns. Chuck presided over the National Rifle Association conventions. At the end of each, he would pick up a rifle and yell "from my cold dead hands." Holy Moses!

I called Chuck when I heard the news. He sent me this lovely letter, dated September 10, 2002, which showed true courage in the face of an enemy that couldn't be vanquished with a gun.

Dear Kirk:

I want you to know I have your message expressing your concern about the announcement I made recently about my health: you've warmed my heart. I accept your prayers gratefully. I, too, respect our differences but the times we've spent together transcend them. I'll never forget them.

I'm not sure I entirely deserve such an outpouring of good wishes from so many people, but I'm taking them all to heart.

Of all the messages I've received, the following from a longtime friend has been the funniest. I thought you might enjoy it. What he wrote was, "Just my luck! The one big-shot that ever remembered my name tells me he may forget it. I find that unacceptable."

Meanwhile, please accept my thanks for your warm support and goodwill. As William Shakespeare said, "Fear not, all will yet be well."

As ever,
Chuck

ANNE:

Never in my wildest dreams as a child could I have imagined the trajectory of my life. Kirk and I have been so blessed, and it has been our privilege to share our good fortune where we care the most. Kirk is forever grateful to St. Lawrence University, and he has funded full scholarships for minority students. There were no African American students in his day, so he leans heavily in favor of those applicants. We support the performing and visual arts because they are vital to a civilized society. In addition to groundbreaking plays, our Kirk Douglas Theatre has workshops and gives performances for children.

Because we are so hands-on with our giving, we don't give blanket funds to a charity or nonprofit. We ask for a list of the most urgent needs and then usually underwrite the most expensive. Recently, we gave Children's Hospital of Los Angeles a multimillion dollar surgical robot that is revolutionary in correcting urological problems quickly and with shortened recovery time. They named it Spartacus.

I like the answer Kirk gave when asked why we are so passionate about our philanthropic work: "What else do you do with your money? You give it away to people who need it. You help them. It feels so good I think it's selfish."

KIRK:

If imitation is the sincerest form of flattery, my son Michael has made me inordinately proud with his devotion to charitable causes. On my ninety-fifth birthday, December 9, 2011, Michael wrote me a letter in which he said he was funding a playground in Israel in my honor. It was a thoughtful and generous gift. He knew how good it would make me feel.

Michael and I have a very close relationship. It was not always that way. We explored our evolution as parent and child in a 2005 HBO documentary called *A Father . . . A Son: Once Upon a Time in Hollywood*. It's an extraordinarily honest—at times funny, at others painful—look at our family dynamic. All of my boys, my wife Anne, and "our ex-wife" Diana are among those weighing in.

Was I a good father? It's a question I posed to Michael in the documentary and many times since. That's why this handwritten letter from him is so precious to me:

12/9/11

Happy Birthday Dad,

Wow 95! What do you get someone who has everything, including wisdom and the love of his family? Well as I mentioned in R.Y., I'm going to sponsor the 401ST playground of the Douglas Foundation at Kfar Chabad, in Anne and your name. It just seemed so appropriate, with the organizations 95th trip of young Jews from the Ukraine and Bella Russ, to Israel in your 95th year.

You ask me "was I a good father?" You are a

setling the bar so high

Michael

Happy Birthday Dad,

Wow 95! What do you get someone who has everything, including wisdom and the love of his family? Well as I mentioned in N.Y., I'm going to sponsor the 401st playground of the Douglas Foundation at the Kfar Chabad in Anne and your name. It just seemed so appropriate, with the organization's 95th trip of young Jews from the Ukraine and Bella Russe, to Israel in your 95th year.

You ask me "<u>was</u> I a good father?" You <u>are</u> a good father! I could not be more proud of you and how you have conducted your life.

Little Issur to Kirk Douglas was an incredible achievement, but your third act is truly inspirational. I love you Dad, you make me proud to be your son. Thank you for setting the bar so high.

Michael

afterword

ANNE:

I have decided to let my husband—the celebrated actor, producer, author, philanthropist, centenarian—have the last word. After all, getting me to share my side of our marriage was his idea, and now he can write whether he still thinks it was a good one.

KIRK:

Thank you, darling. This process was easy for me. I've always loved talking about myself, and you've always loved talking about me. That's one of the secrets to our long and happy marriage.

Looking back at our many decades together from your viewpoint has been a revelation. Your stories have given me a fresh perspective on many of our experiences, and I thank you for talking about them and how they affected you.

For those readers who worry that the world we live in is a mess, I hope you will see that every generation faces challenges. Somehow we get past them.

Thank you to all—participants and readers—who have taken the journey with us. And thank you to everyone who allowed us to reprint their correspondence for this book.

We wish everyone a love as enriching as ours and a life filled with sharing and caring.

acknowledgments

THE OLDER I GET, THE FASTER THINGS SEEM TO MOVE. *Kirk and Anne* was merely an idea in April 2016, when Anne first brought me our correspondence. I was amazed to relive the emotions of our early years of courtship and marriage. That became the backbone of our book. I am grateful to my wife for being such a prudent caretaker of our memories.

Now, we would like to appreciate those who have shared the journey with us.

Marcia Newberger, who has handled my publicity for years, was the biggest help. She coordinated all the letters and interviewed me. Our friend David Bender interviewed Anne without my presence. She told him stories I had forgotten or never knew at all. I thank him for recording them.

I must thank Running Press senior editor Cindy De La Hoz for her help in readying the manuscript, and for her professional eye in selecting photos to illustrate our story.

My assistant, Grace Medinger, as always, motivated me to keep going and eased the process with her computer skills and her transcription of hours of interviews. I appreciate her contribution to the process.

Lastly, my wife, Anne. Thank you, darling, for taking the leap of faith to write this book with me. I am grateful for your love, support, and encouragement.

I would also like to acknowledge my family and especially the grandchildren, who give Anne and me such joy. I hope they won't be shocked by the intensity of the love letters their Oma and Pappy wrote! Perhaps they will come to value, even in this technology-driven world of instant communication, the joy of writing and receiving non-electronic letters—particularly when it comes to love.

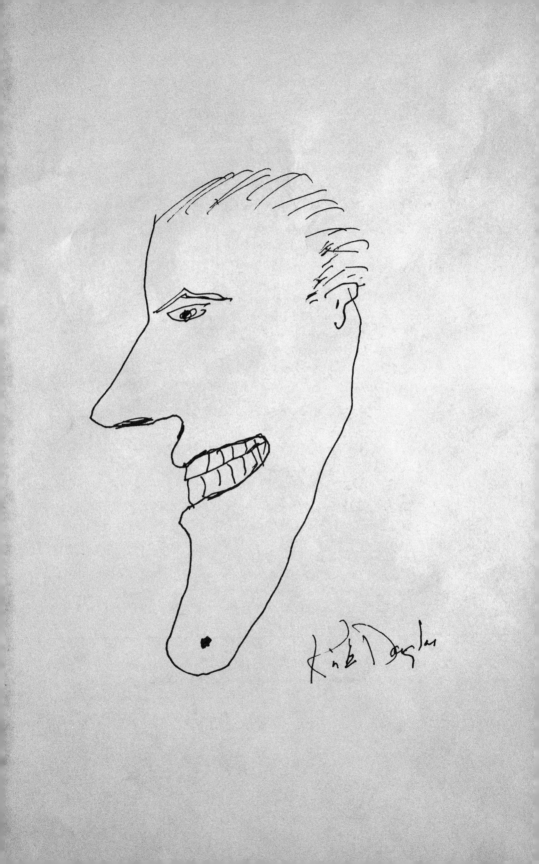

photo credits

Cover: *Arthur Zinn*
Page 6: *Christopher Briscoe*
Page 40: *UPI, Bettmann Newsphotos*
Page 127: *Universal Pictures Archives*
Page 143: *Academy of Motion Picture Arts and Sciences*
Page 220: *Larry Dale Gordon*
Insert page 6, top: *George Keeley*
Insert page 7, top right: *Arthur Zinn*
Insert page 13, top left: *Roddy McDowell*
Insert page 15, bottom: *Michael Jacobs*
Insert page 16: *Michael Jacobs*
Insert page 17, top and middle: *Michael Jacobs;* **bottom right:** *Christopher Briscoe*

All other photos from the Douglas Collection

letter credits

Tony Curtis: *From the Estate of Tony Curtis*
Burt Lancaster: *By permission of the Lancaster family*
Robin Williams: *The Robin Williams Trust*
Henry Kissinger: *Reprinted with the permission of Henry A. Kissinger*
Charlton Heston: *© Charlton Heston 2002. Permission by Heston Family Estate*
Nancy Reagan: *Ronald Reagan Presidential Foundation Institute*
Billy Crystal: *By permission of Billy Crystal*
Robert Downey Jr.: *Exxie Unlimited, Inc.*
Barack Obama: *Letter provided by the Office of the Former President Barack Obama*
John Wayne: *Batjac Productions, Inc.*
Harry Cohn: *Courtesy of Columbia Pictures*